VK p 40   4-28-70

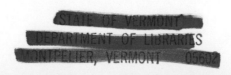

WARFARE

BOOKS BY ROBERT LECKIE

Warfare
Ordained
The Wars of America
Challenge for the Pacific
These Are My Heroes
With Fire and Sword (edited with Quentin Reynolds)
Strong Men Armed
Conflict
The March to Glory
Marines!
Lord, What a Family!
Helmet for My Pillow

FOR YOUNGER READERS

Great American Battles
The Battle for Iwo Jima
The Story of Football
The Story of World War Two
The Story of World War One
The War in Korea
The Big Game
Keeper Play!
Stormy Voyage

WARFARE

by

Robert Leckie

1817

HARPER & ROW, PUBLISHERS
New York, Evanston, and London

355.02
L46/w
1970

FIRST EDITION

LIBRARY OF CONGRESS CATALOG CARD NUMBER: 70-85282

To Russell Davis,
dear friend and old buddy

CONTENTS

ILLUSTRATIONS

AUTHOR'S PREFACE

Surely this is madness, to write now of war, especially of the institution itself, when all the world is sick of war and when America is agonized and divided over the war in Vietnam. And yet, perhaps that is exactly why such a book is needed. Everywhere there is war or talk of war, and yet, so few people (the statesmen included) seem to understand it: how it starts, how it spreads, how difficult it is to stop.

Perhaps this is because throughout time and everywhere in the world, men have generally scorned war as a subject fit for study. True, there have been some philosophers, theologians, social scientists, diplomats, jurists, and even (God spare the mark!) some generals who have reflected and written about the institution; but in the main, men have regarded military history as "a dreary compendium of maps and maneuvers, of calibers and compass bearings." As the French military writer Monteilhet said: "The noise of battles fills history . . . but no light shines upon the ways in which people become soldiers." What a tragic contradiction! In all of 5,500 years of recorded history, there have not been 230 years of peace; in our own country's career there have not been 20 years in which one of our armed services was not engaged in some military campaign or operation—and yet mankind in general and ourselves in particular persist in the delusion that "peace" is normal and war abnormal. Even if war were abnormal, that would be no reason for refusing to study it. Medical science certainly did not improve the physical well-being of mankind by studying good health. Obviously, to detest or denounce a

xi

disease as pacifists do with war, is not enough; to get rid of it or control it one must understand it.

Pacifism, incidentally, is a second explanation of why Americans abhor the study of war. We are now the most martial people on the globe and our history, which runs exactly concurrent with the annals of modern arms, demonstrates that we are perhaps the "fightingest" society since Rome, yet we still bear in our bloodstream a strong pacifist strain. The reassuring myth of "peace-loving America" is not yet dead. It continues to flourish in face of the fact that it was by war, not by peace, that we learned to govern ourselves, won our independence, pushed our frontiers from ocean to ocean, abolished chattel slavery, became a Far Eastern power, entered international affairs and finally accepted the leadership of the free world. Yet, few colleges offer books on our wars in any of their history courses. As Allan Nevins says, such studies "have been dismissed as drum-and-trumpet history, fit only for the adolescent mind." And this is because of an inbred pacifism, a habit of mind which is every bit as dangerous as aggression. (I do not say "as militarism," because militarism is not the opposite of pacifism. Militarism is the opposite of civilianism; it is the domination of the state by the military men rather than the civilian, a condition which has not quite come to pass in America.) Both pacifism and aggression are extreme attitudes, and both take an unrealistic view of human nature. The pacifist trusts men too much, and the aggressor trusts them too little. And when a pacifist says he will not fight he invites attack from the aggressor who likes, not to fight, but to push people around. The pacifist, an idealist, is a lamb who seems to believe that his gentle bleats will induce the lion to lie down with him; the aggressor, who calls himself a "realist," is a lion who believes the lamb is his meat.

Fortunately for America, the aggressor (a better word would be "bully") has seldom if ever held the upper hand. I say "fortunately" because any man who wants to "solve things" by filling the air with atom bombs, as I have heard many aggressive people propose, is simply beyond reason. He is the man who thinks of victory in terms of annihilation, who "makes a desert and calls it peace." Happily, his influence rarely extends beyond his own dining room.

Pacifists, however, that is to say, people who preach non-violence and renounce all recourse to force of arms, are most influential. They are educated and articulate, even though they do not seem to understand the contradictions inherent in their absolutism. When they denounce war as a murderous anachronism, they do not realize that they are hardly better than a doctor trying to destroy a disease by calling it names; when they suggest that war should be "outlawed," they fail to understand that the very fact of war presupposes a breakdown of law.

Pacifism is not always clear-sighted. When Gandhian non-violence was employed for the "passive invasion" of Goa, that is, an offensive march by unarmed people, the applauding pacifists did not seem to understand that they were cheering another form of coercion. "Passive resistance" may be non-violent, but so are other successful forms of coercion such as excommunication, ostracism or economic boycott. Nor do pacifiists think out the consequences of their attitude. Leo Tolstoy had the courage to see that his pacifism led inevitably to vegetarianism: he could not in conscience eat the flesh of any animal deprived of its life. The consequence of this vegetarianism which is the corollary of pacifism, however, is that the beasts which we do not kill and eat will not only cease to be a major source of our food but will, by continuing to breed, emerge as a formidable competitor for a world food supply already dangerously inadequate.

A second consequence of pacifism is that by naively believing it will exert a moral influence over an aggressor it has actually been just as productive of war as its unlovely opposite. War came in Korea because America returned to pacifism after World War II. We dismantled the greatest fighting force ever assembled, and then, after our leaders publicly proclaimed our unwillingness to defend South Korea, the Communists crossed the 38th parallel. No one was more surprised than Joseph Stalin and his North Korean puppets when we rushed back to battle to stop them. There, of course, is the surest and most melancholy formula for war: the situation in which one nation mistakenly believes another nation will not fight.

Because the pacifists among us are generally more articulate than the aggressors, it is their voice to which the enemy, always eager to detect signs of weakness in his victims, invariably listens. Hitler sneered, "Americans are too soft to fight like heroes," and lived to hear the crash of American bombs on Berlin. Premier Nikita Khrushchev of the Soviet Union remarked, "Americans are too liberal to fight," and then was compelled to crawl away from the Cuban Confrontation. Because the Japanese attack on Pearl Harbor unified the United States as never before, and brought utter retribution upon the head of Nippon, it has usually been considered the military blunder without parallel; and yet, Pearl Harbor would not have been bombed had the Japanese not been convinced that America would weary of a long war. This mistaken assumption was in great part due to pacifist propaganda among us; and in this, the Japanese were only joining a long and disillusioned list of enemies. From King George III to Lord Liverpool through Santa Anna and Aguinaldo to Kaiser Bill, Hitler, Mussolini, Tojo, Stalin, Kim Il Sung, Mao Tsetung and, presently, Ho Chi Minh, the enemies of this country have based their strategy on the myth of the "soft" American. And this is chiefly the result of pacifist propaganda here.

Worse, it has not only deluded them, but ourselves as well. Generation after generation of American boys have been spoon-fed on Fourth of July oratorical pap about "this great

and peace-loving nation," only to be marched off to the holo-
causts and blood baths which have given us our Memorial
Days, our Veterans and Pearl Harbor Days. We have all been
born and bred to pacifism, or at least to that hypocritical cant
which says that we are not a warrior people.

When I was born, the Great War had been ended only two
years. When I was in kindergarten the Marines were fighting
in the "Banana Wars" of the Caribbean, but as I grew up the
only things I ever heard about war was that it was "the bunk"
or else the evil means by which bloated bankers and munitions-makers battened on the blood of their countrymen. By
the time I was ten the pacifist reaction was so strong that the
words "honor" and "glory" had all but vanished from the
American vocabulary; but in that same year Japan invaded
Manchuria. At fourteen I wrote a hopeful poem ending with
the voice of God proclaiming, "War has been taken away,"
and it did not disturb either my teacher or me to learn, a few
days later, that Mussolini had attacked Ethiopia. What the
poem meant, I suppose, was that war had been taken away
from *us,* that the Almighty had exempted our noble race from
this recurrent curse of mankind. In Europe, of course, the
pernicious custom would continue. I think that this was the
general attitude in our country then, and that this explains
why my friends and my teachers and I were not too excited
when Nazi Germany rushed to rearm, when Hitler reoccupied
the Rhineland, when the Spanish Civil War raised the curtain
on a bloody dress rehearsal for World War II, and, finally,
when the Fuehrer began to bully the Anglo-French into ac-
ceding to his territorial demands.

In 1938, the year of the great Anglo-French sellout at
Munich, I was graduated from high school. Now, looking at
my yearbook, I see that none of my classmates, answering the
question, "What is your secret ambition?" wanted to be a
general or an admiral. The same is true of every yearbook I
had ever seen. To wish to be a professional soldier in those

days was worse than unthinkable; it was contrary to the "American way"; it was adolescent; and young men who enrolled in the college R.O.T.C. courses were jeered at as "Boy Scouts" motivated by nothing nobler than the wish to wear a uniform, like any bellhop or theater usher.

In those depression days, two of my friends dropped out of school, one to join the Navy, the other to enter the Army. Why did they enlist? Because they couldn't get a job. They signed up for "three hots and a flop" and twenty-one dollars a day once a month. If anyone had suggested to them that they might one day fight a battle, they would have been horrified; and, in fact, when World War II did come in Europe and with it the munitions orders that broke the back of the depression, my friends came tumbling out of the service to avail themselves of these newfound opportunities for employment.

Events, of course, ultimately shattered the pacifist delusion that war may be avoided by turning away from it, and America entered World War II to help defeat the Axis; after which, just as she was crawling back into the pacifist womb, she came to realize that Communism was as dark a despotism as Fascism; and with that the Cold War began and in 1949 Red China appeared in history. A year later, America was fighting the Red Chinese, as well as their North Korean allies, in Korea. Four years after that, when my oldest son was in kindergarten, the French bastion at Dienbienphu in what is now North Vietnam fell to the Communist Vietminh; and with that defeat, our own escalating involvement in Vietnam began.

Since then our country has made military interventions in Lebanon, the Congo and the Dominican Republic; and our support of Israel in the Middle East might at any time involve us in a shooting war against the Arabs. Everywhere in the world, where the forces of the open society confront those of the closed society, there is a possibility of war; and that confrontation will probably continue until one or both sides come to the conclusion that war is no longer a useful instrument of policy.

This is how the world stands in the present year 1969. At forty-eight years of age, I have known only a few years when the world was at peace; at twenty, my oldest son has not known a single warless day. War, then, not peace, has been the norm of our existence. War, it would seem, is worth a word or two, even a little book like this.

ROBERT LECKIE

Mountain Lakes, New Jersey
August 7, 1969

WARFARE

1. THEN AND NOW

Men are fighting creatures, and it is probable that they have been killing each other since they first came into competition or conflict with one another. According to the Bible, Cain committed the first murder: he killed his brother, Abel. When, we know not; how, we know not; nor do we know for certain if the Biblical account is not actually an allegory representing the age-old conflict between the pastoral people, as manifested in Cain, the keeper of sheep, and the agricultural, as expressed in Abel, the tiller of the soil. We do know, however, that the earliest known specimen of our probable ancestry— the fossil *Homo habilis* discovered in 1964—was a murdered child. Therefore, as long as 2,000,000 years ago our probable ancestors were not only hunting and killing animals ten or twenty times their size, they were also killing one another.

Apart from some of the social insects, which actually wage war, it is rare for other animals to kill others of their kind. They fight, of course, but seldom to the death. We seem to be a special species. Awkward, slow afoot, thin-skinned, armed by nature with puny claws, teeth and jaws, we should have long ago expired were it not for the splendid psychological equipment seated between our ears. Our heads conceived of weapons, which our hands (unique because of the grasping power of our thumbs) then made, and our hearts were constant enough to enable us to wield them face to face with those snarling, roaring creatures who were so many times our natural superiors as fighters.

Indeed, in fashioning his first weapons, primitive man imi-

3

tated the horns, claws and tusks which were the natural equipment of such hunting animals as the lion, tiger and wolf. He also copied their tactics of stalk, pounce and retreat. As he became more sophisticated, so did his weapons, so that to the fist-ax of the sort that may have dispatched little *Homo habilis* were added war clubs, battle-axes and swords; missile weapons such as javelins and thrown-spears, the arrow propelled by hand- or foot-drawn bow, darts hurled or blown through blowpipes; and, finally, thrusting spears.

With these weapons, primitive men waged war; and as much as their weaponry might be improved, their tactics of stalk-pounce-and-retreat remained the same. If the theft of a cow or the abduction of a woman sent tribe against tribe, the technique of sudden ambush or the dawn raid seldom varied. Even among the American Indians, "war" was hardly more than a series of raids and ambushes. The idea of mass and maneuver, of a war of attrition or of siege, apparently did not occur to them. If there was a "battle," that is, a shock between opposing lines, it was over quickly; perhaps in a matter of minutes. Indian warfare most often was characterized by the hunter's chief tactic of surprise: a stealthy night approach upon some sleeping village, the war whoop, a sudden rush— and the tomahawk in the brain. At least among the Iroquois, victory was usually celebrated by eating the slain enemy in the sight of his survivors, after which the village was burned and the victors withdrew with their trophies and such prisoners as might serve them as slaves or amuse them as objects of torture.

In such warfare, physical strength would count for much; and it is a fact that the dreaded Iroquois, while not exceptionally big men, were unusually agile. Like all primitives, the Indians fought on foot. Horses were not available to them until thousands of years after primitive man civilized himself by war; to be exact, at the end of the 1500s, when Spanish mares and stallions turned loose in the Southwest sired the mustangs and broncos which were to become the mounts of the Plains Indians. When the Indians did become mobile, their prowess as mounted marksmen made them formidable foes indeed. How different American history might have been, if the mounted Indians of the prairies could have been led by a cavalry genius of the stature of Genghis Khan.

In this first stage of fighting known as Primitive Warfare, nomads such as the Plains Indians were usually better warriors than the settled food-gatherers; and this confirms the Cain-slew-Abel allegory that the herdsman, the hardy dweller of the desert or the steppes, will usually defeat the tiller living in peaceful plains and valleys. It is just because the nomad had a harder environment to conquer that he became the hardier warrior. He also profited from a stimulating climate; and the vast distances which he covered as a matter of daily living taught him to organize and specialize for international war. In a word, the nomad was born and bred to raid, just as the dweller of the seashore was drawn to piracy, and the unfortunate agriculturist was actually undone by his sedentary life and the delights of his smiling valleys.

In our own technological times, the extremes of heat and cold probably do not influence a people's martial spirit. Among primitives, however, extreme climates tended to make for non-warlike people. People dwelling behind secure mountain barriers or within inaccessible forests also tended to be peaceable; but if the climate was stimulating, as with the forest-dwelling Iroquois, they might have been among the most ferocious. It seems a fact that soft countries make soft men, as Herodotus, the father of history, suggested when he closed his *History of the Persian Wars* by reciting the incident when the Great King's courtiers pleaded: "O Cyrus, come now, let us quit this land wherein we dwell—for it is a scant land and a rugged—and let us choose ourselves some other better country. . . ." Then Cyrus, who did not greatly esteem their counsel, told them they might do so if they liked—but he warned them not to expect in that case to continue rulers, but to prepare for being ruled by others—soft countries gave birth to soft men—there was no region which produced very delightful fruits, and at the same time men of a warlike spirit.

Of primitive men, then, it was the restless wanderer, not the settled food-gatherer, who triumphed; and it is to him that we owe civilization. It might very well have been that the warrior's desire to perpetuate the glory of his deeds in song and story was the original impetus for written language, the arrival of which is usually considered the beginning of civilized society.

Therefore, as history dawned in the light of writing, war entered its second phase, one which may be called Historic Warfare. This second stage is a vast period covering roughly 6,000 years and extending to about 1500 A.D. During this period weapons and tactics changed. Missile weapons such as javelins and arrows tended to give way before piercing or penetrating arms such as swords and spears, the horse and later the saddle appeared, the size of the war band increased, discipline grew stronger, the range of specialties widened and the tactics of pounce and retreat were superseded by those of mass and maneuver. In a word, war became more efficient and therefore more destructive.

Historic Warfare seems to have had two distinguishing characteristics: it was personal and it was landlocked. By personal, I mean that the warriors of the contending armies usually confronted each other face-to-face and fought hand-to-hand. Combat was in fact so personal that Alexander is supposed to have ordered his men to shave so that their beards would not offer handholds to the enemy. True enough, there were archers and slingers who fired missiles from a distance, but these weapons were rarely regarded as the decisive arm. Flights of arrows and showers of stones usually preceded an attack or attempted to cover a retreat, and they were often deflected by the shields of the enemy. The soldiers who fired them were considered auxiliary troops: either skirmishers, that is, individual soldiers operating on their own in front of their advancing army, and therefore capable only of a harassing effect, or massed in bands stationed on the wings or to the rear. The true decision in battle, however, was given by the main body of troops wielding swords and spears, fighting on foot or on horseback. Such soldiers saw each other, struck at each other within arm's length, heard each other's shouts and screams, and felt the enemy's hot blood run out upon their flesh. War, then, was personal. Because it was, battle was brief. The very phrase "to carry the day" is suggestive of this, indicating that the charge which overwhelmed the enemy, or the unflinching stand that shattered the charge, were both of short duration; and a battle seldom lasted for more than a few hours. It might be renewed the next day, but even then, a battle during the period of Historic Warfare was an event to be measured by the hour.

Historic Warfare was also landlocked—it might even be called "local"—because it was between or among civilized peoples who had not yet learned to navigate the oceans. True, there were naval battles such as the Greek victory over the Persians at Salamis in 480 B.C., and the Vikings of the ninth and tenth centuries seem to have been a society of seafaring soldiers. Actually, however, battles such as Salamis or the Roman-Carthaginian sea fights were always fought close to land within the relative calm of inland seas such as the Mediterranean. In fact, they hardly even "sailed," because their warships were mainly oared galleys. The Vikings, of course, were plain and simple pirates, bloody plunderers whose success depended upon the helplessness of the towns and monasteries they reached by ascending the rivers of Europe. No one would think of the Vikings as a "sea power" in the same sense that Great Britain was *the* sea power of the last century. With the notable exception of Alexander, not many conquerors of the age of Historic Warfare seem to have understood the importance of sea power; and this would appear to be simply because even the most civilized societies were still landlocked.

As a result, they got at each other by land. All the conquering peoples of the age of Historic Warfare—Egyptian and Assyrian, Persian, Greek and Roman, pagan barbarian of steppe and forest, Christian European or Moslem Turk and Arab, as well as the fierce horsemen of Mongolia—all of them walked or rode to the battle. Moreover, their "world" was a rather small one, consisting chiefly of Europe, the Middle East and India. Our own Western Hemisphere, the vast Eurasian steppe now comprising most of the Soviet Union, the Far East, most of Africa south of the Sahara and the islands of Oceania were unknown to them. It was not until the 1200s, about two centuries or more before the period ended, that the Mongol horsemen made themselves an actual, if unwelcome, link between East and West.

Historic Warfare, then, even though more destructive than the Primitive Warfare which it succeeded, was still more restrained than the Modern Warfare which was to follow it. This was because of the limitations of personal combat and landlocked war. Personal, war was limited in time; landlocked, it was limited in space. A third limitation seems to spring from Historic Warfare's first characteristic of being personal. This is that all weapons and means of military movement were driven by muscle power, either of men or of animals. While the bows of the early Egyptians and the siege engines of the Assyrians were based on a mechanical principle, they nevertheless required muscle power to cock them. When firearms and chemicals supplanted muscle-powered weapons for striking, when animal-powered vehicles gave way to those driven by wind, steam, gasoline and electricity, and when the entire world became converted into an arena for war, then the more restrained era of Historic Warfare was replaced by the third awful and unchecked age of destruction which is our own period of Modern War.

Like its predecessor, this age also has two chief characteristics: firearms and mobility. The first made weapons more destructive, the second made their range world-wide.

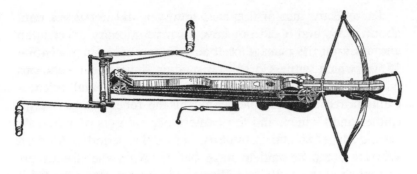

A kind of transitional weapon between the longbow (muscle-powered) and the musket (firearm), the crossbow was cocked by winding a winch with one foot on its attached steel arm.

It is difficult to say exactly when firearms first appeared. It has been claimed that gunpowder existed in China as early as the first century, and perhaps 500 years before that the Greeks were pouring their terrifying "Greek fire"—an oily, tarry combustible—on the heads of invaders from land and sea. There is also a legend which puts the inventions of firearms in the year 1320, when a German monk named Berthold Schwarz, a dabbler in the forbidden mystico-chemical delights of alchemy, sought to make gold by boiling a mixture of sulfur, saltpeter, quicksilver, oil and lead, and succeeded only in cooking up explosions so violent that they sometimes wrecked his laboratory. Here was not gold but gunpowder. However, this curious and disobedient monk, whose last name, "Schwarz" or "Black," actually was a nickname derived from his habit of practicing the "black art" of alchemy (and also, one suspects, from his frequently singed appearance), was *not* the man who first thought of propelling a ball through a metal tube by exploding a charge of gunpowder behind it. Whether we wish to bless or to curse the true author of firearms, we do not have the gentleman's name. Suffice it to say that within eight years of Black Berthold's opening blasts, the French had cannon; and in another twenty years the seafaring English were firing them from their ships.

The effective use of firearms, however, did not begin until about 1450, and it did not have its revolutionary effect upon warfare until the passage of that momentous century (1450–1550) which witnessed so many other shattering revolutions in art, literature and philosophy, in religion and science. Cannon had to be complemented by the rebellions of Martin Luther and Galileo, and the exploratory voyages of Vasco da Gama, Magellan and Columbus, before the period of Modern Warfare could be said to have begun. After the discoverers had mapped the world and charted the oceans, after the spirit of inquiry had shattered the concept of a static society governed by immutable laws, the restless, rising kingdoms of Europe could sail forth—gun in hand—to occupy the Americas, the Pacific and Africa, and to spread their influence over the ancient civilized peoples of Russia, the Middle East, India and China. Certainly, all this was not accomplished by firearms and soldiers alone. Europe's influence was also spread by missionaries, traders, sailors, writers, artists and administrators. Nevertheless, it was firearms following in the wake of the navigators which gave the world a world civilization.

The development of artillery made possible the creation of those strong national kingdoms erected on the crumbled keeps of feudalism. Because it was so expensive, artillery soon became the monopoly of kings seeking to undo the power of the barons. A few centuries later, Louis XIV of France would mark his cannon with the boast: "The last argument of kings." In fact, it was their first argument, the one that knocked down the baronial strongholds and compelled stiff-necked nobles to submit to national dynasties. "Where are now those numerous robber castles, built on high mountains, in which not a few shamefully robbing and burning murderers, preserving themselves safely, not only made whole territories unsafe, but even defied the highest and crowned heads? Have they not been intimidated by the guns, like chickens, and are their residences not turned into stone-heaps and dens of owls, snakes, and bad spirits?" Thus did a certain Captain Michael Mieth, in the service of the Holy Roman Emperor, salute his beloved guns in the year 1683. True enough, like all "cannon-cockers" before and since, artillerist Mieth may have been exaggerating the results of his cannonade; but it is nevertheless undeniable that the centralizing authority in Europe, not its opposite, was better served by firearms.

Not quite so obvious as the destructive power of firearms was the equally dreadful fact that they were impersonal. Men might now be maimed or murdered from a distance, and their unobserved agony or death throes would therefore leave their assailants unmoved. Result: war grew less compassionate, if one may so describe man's cruelest calling. Another result: battle was prolonged as the fire of artillery or massed muskets had an inhibiting effect on a general's desire for the decisive shock. As the combat of armies came to be measured in days rather than hours, the problems of keeping them supplied and fed in the field also increased. This military specialty, known as logistics, i.e., the supply, sheltering and movement of troops, was further complicated by the mercenary soldier's custom of taking the field accompanied by "camp followers": wives, children, servants, purveyors of food and drink and prostitutes. In the early part of the seventeenth century the ordinary soldier in the army of Count Tilly of France had at least one woman and a boy at his service, a lieutenant rated five servants and a colonel eighteen. In those days, when plunder was a soldier's actual wage, as the men grew heavy with booty they hired drudges to carry it for them. Thus, in the Thirty Years' War, an army of 38,000 fighting men dragged a huge tail of 127,000 camp followers behind it.

The armies of early Modern Warfare were truly devouring dragons, leaving the countryside they traversed sere and scorched; and at no time was this more apparent than in the Thirty Years' War. It was unfortunate for Europe that at the very moment when firearms made war more destructive than before, the passions of Christian men everywhere were inflamed by the Protestant Reformation and the Catholic Counter-Reformation that followed it. The spark of religious fervor (or fanaticism) that exploded the Thirty Years' War set the Protestant princes of Germany against the Catholic Emperor Ferdinand, and three decades later, after it had followed the inexorable logic of war whereby the exalted gives way to the base and the ideological to the material or political, it had left Central Europe a hideous ruin. So dreadful were these twin scourges of firearm and fanaticism that the German Empire, which, exclusive of the Netherlands and Bohemia, numbered 21,000,000 inhabitants in 1618, had diminished to less than 13,500,000 in 1648.

As great as had been the carnage, greater still was the revulsion which followed it. Civilized men drew back from this new horror of unlimited war. As in our own day when all mankind came under the grim shadow of the Mushroom Cloud, men began to consider ways and means of limiting or controlling war. None of them, however, advocated outlawing it. Instead, they recommended moderation, preaching a rule of reason. The Swiss jurist Emmerich de Vattel, realizing to what lengths men armed with firearms could now push their belief that their own cause was good and the enemy's evil, introduced an entirely new concept of war and codified it in a book called *The Law of Nations*.

Vattel began by insisting that it was impossible to pass judgment on the justice of any given war, simply because neither side accepted or held itself accountable to any judge. Thus, from the impossibility of attempting to judge the cause or the purpose of a war, it was more sensible merely to pass judgment on the *means* of waging it. To be just, war must be waged by certain moderating rules. The first of these was simply to avoid what we now call "escalation" of a conflict, to refrain from employing more and more destructive means.

As Vattel observed, if one side uses poison, the other will retaliate in kind; if another begins to burn cities, his enemy will also pick up the torch. When this happens, war becomes unlimited or total; neutrals are drawn into the fray; and the doors of peace are slammed shut, one by one.

It is surely one of the great marvels of history that the quarreling dynasties of the age of Absolute Kings did in fact try to limit their wars. They restrained themselves both as to ends and as to means, seeking neither the total prostration of their enemy nor the employment of more and more destructive weapons. Naturally, there were other limiting factors, chief among them the high costs of maintaining paid professional armies and the high casualties caused by firearm-battle. In those days of what is called "linear warfare," that is, "lines" of soldiers two or three ranks deep advancing openly upon each other and firing musket volleys as they closed, the carnage could be frightful. At Malplaquet in 1709 the Allied army of 90,000 men suffered losses of 33 percent, of which 11,000 to 15,000 were killed. As late as 1758, in the Battle of Zorndorf, a Russian army of 42,000 men lost half its number in killed and wounded, a slaughter which Colonel Hoffman Nickerson claims to be "a world's record for a field army during a single day's fighting in which the defeated side is neither crushed nor unresistingly massacred."

Obviously, it was folly incarnate to spend so much money on an army that might be mutilated in an hour or two. Soldiers were much too expensive to be risked in pitched firearm-battle. Therefore, battle was now to be avoided rather than sought. Naturally, battles occurred; the very engagements just cited were fought during the era of limited war. In practice, however, a good general would enter an army-to-army contest only after he had maneuvered his opponent into an untenable position or a frustrated frame of mind.

Maneuver, then, became the premium skill; and there is a second reason for this. Because of the horror of the Thirty

Years' War, armies no longer made war on civil populations. Pillaging was prohibited. Instead, an army either supplied itself by requisitioning local products for which cash payment was made, or by the "magazine" system.

Magazines were depots established in fortresses and fortified towns in the army's rear and supplied by supply trains from the home base. In turn, they supplied the advancing army. However, an army was limited to about seven marches from the nearest magazine and about two from the nearest field ovens. Armies of that time also dwelt fairly comfortably in tents, which, of course, had to be struck and packed whenever the march was resumed. Obviously, then, these armies were ponderous affairs, huge martial centipedes toiling along the dusty roads weighted down by tentage, artillery, wagon trains and the customary horde of camp followers. To be able to maneuver them surely, to feint against the enemy and withdraw, to come upon his rear or to menace his supply lines— in a word, to confuse and distract and exhaust him—was indeed a high skill. As Sir John Fortescue has observed: "To force an enemy to consume his own supplies was much, to compel him to supply his opponents was more, to take up winter-quarters in his territory was very much more. Thus to enter an enemy's borders and keep him marching backwards and forwards for weeks without giving him a chance of striking a blow was in itself no small success, and success of a kind which galled inferior generals, such as William of Orange, to desperation and so to disaster."

It was thus, then, that those dreadful bogeymen of the modern world—the Absolute Kings—supplanted wars of annihilation with wars of attrition. Rather than crush their enemy, they sought to exhaust him. It was not so much that they understood that to destroy one member of the royal club was to upset its balance, but also that, money being scarce, they found it cheaper to defeat the foe by depleting his treasury than by meeting him in pitched battle. Thus, when the treasury ran dry, one or another of the contestants would sue for a negotiated peace. And that was exactly what happened in our own War of the Revolution.

It remained for another revolution, the French, to set loose the monster of unlimited war which the Absolute Kings, for all their tyranny, had wisely sought to chain. In 1793, by a decree of the Convention, the famous *levée en masse* placed the entire French nation on a footing of total war. Because that decree was so momentous for mankind, it is quoted here in full.

From this moment until that in which our enemies shall have been driven from the territory of the Republic, all Frenchmen are permanently requisitioned for service in the armies.

The young men shall fight; the married men shall forge weapons and transport supplies; the women will make tents and clothes and will serve in the hospitals; the children will make up old linen into lint; the old men will have themselves carried into the public squares to rouse the courage of the fighting men, to preach the unity of the Republic and hatred against Kings.

The public buildings shall be turned into barracks, the public square into munition factories, the earthen floors of cellars shall be treated with lye to extract saltpeter.

All firearms of suitable caliber shall be turned over to the troops; the interior shall be policed with shotguns and with cold steel.

All saddle horses shall be seized for the cavalry; all draft horses not employed in cultivation will draw the artillery and supply wagons.

There it is, as thrilling as a bugle call, as defiant as a roll of drums, and in the way of the French at war, so practical and precise. But what a dreadful irony! To end tyranny the French nation was "permanently requisitioned" for the army. In the name of freedom, a new form of enslavement: *permanent requisition*. Thus, it was out of the womb of Liberty, Equality, and Fraternity that the monster of conscription was born. And it changed warfare.

Once, soldiers had been expensive; now they were cheap. Once, battle had been avoided; now it was sought. Conscription made possible the mass armies of then and now, the mass slaughter of then and now, and it made men so utterly expendable that Napoleon Bonaparte could boast to Metternich: "I spend 30,000 men a month." Why not? There was always the draft to replace his losses. How well might he sneer at the "rosewater war" of the eighteenth century, when he, at the beginning of the nineteenth, had all the conscript blood he needed to turn it stinking scarlet again.

Conscription also put an end to compassion for civilian populations. It was far too costly to maintain mass armies by the civilized custom of paying for supplies or moving them from home via the magazine system. Once again, war was to support war; the countryside was to be plundered. Moreover, all those tents and field ovens, trunks and wagons—the frills and furbelows of what Karl von Clausewitz, the great Prussian military theorist, also derided as "shilly-shally war"—were not only expensive but cumbersome, interfering with the mobility of mass armies now marching rapidly to concentrate for the decisive big battles. So the equipage and the draft animals vanished, men bivouacked in the open, slept in the mud and fought in every kind of weather. The result: they sickened and died, and as many soldiers were lost to the rigors of campaigning as to enemy gunfire. But what matter, when men were so plentiful.

Most tragic of all, conscription made possible the era of *national war*. The draft appeared just at that moment in history when nationalism arose, when the allegiance of the demon which dwells within men was transferred from religious to political ideals. When war had been waged in the interest of some dynasty, for the possession of a province, it aroused little passion in the contestants. But now, being fought for principle, for independence, for national unity, it was by definition a conflict of passion. Every last private in the Revolutionary armies of France now had a stake in spreading the ideals of Liberty, Equality and Fraternity. In France, the appeal to passion which had made the Wars of Religion so hideous, was carefully regulated in the service of the Republic. Once its effectiveness had been demonstrated, Napoleon astutely enrolled it in his own service as emperor, only to be imitated by the rest of Europe as Throne and Altar gradually were supplanted by the Ballot Box.

Conscription, then, actually was the handmaiden of the new religion of Democracy. Faith in Man was supplanting faith in God. The mass-man enrolled in mass-armies was now prepared to make a slaughter which would make previous warfare seem truly scented indeed. Promising political freedom and equality for every man, Democracy also compelled every man to fight for its propagation or defense. The old coin of celestial paradise was replaced by the new one of terrestrial perfection. But if the new coin's obverse side proclaimed One Man and One Ballot, its darker, inverse side said One Man and One Bullet.

Thus, the Democratization of war—the device of the draft by which mass-armies might be raised and inflamed with the spirit of nationalism—was the single great step by which Modern Warfare became so terrible and total. True enough, the ensuing seventeen decades were to witness the arrival of five more revolutions in Modern War, each making it more devastating; but all of these were mere differences in degree. The Democratic Revolution was a difference in *kind*.

The next revolution to follow the Democratic was the Industrial, and its effects were felt most indelibly during our own Civil War. The Napoleonic Wars had been fought before the Industrial Revolution could have its full effect upon war, but by 1860 the uses of steel and steam had made it possible for huge conscript armies to make marvelous slaughter of each other. While the new techniques of mass production were able to equip the mass armies with ever more efficient weapons, the telegraph, the steamboat and the steam locomotive were able to mobilize them and get them at each other's throats more rapidly.

A decade later, and Modern War was overtaken by its fourth revolution: the Managerial. This was the application of business efficiency techniques to the business of war, and it was first manifested by the great success of the Prussian General Staff during the Franco-Prussian War of 1870. The effect of the Managerial Revolution was to encourage the scientific training of officers who would form an administrative organization—or "staff"—through which the chief commander might mass and move his armies. War having been made national and then industrial was now made more efficient. Like the Firearms Revolution, the Managerial Revolution had the intangible effect of making war even more impersonal. Officers trained to think of troops as so many ciphers to be spent or saved, like dollars in the bank or shells in an ammunition depot, inevitably came to disregard the human element in war. It is not too much to suggest that the awful carnage now known as World War I might have been far less hideous had it not been for this calculating and impersonal habit of mind cultivated by the Managerial Revolution. Far behind the lines, away from the stench of death, the mud and the lice and the bloated rats, beyond the sound of shells crashing and the feel of the trench trembling, generals and field marshals in polished leather and gleaming brass assembled at their headquarters like so many well-groomed members of the board of directors, there to partake of epicurean meals while deciding how many thousands of fathers and sons, husbands and brothers would have to be considered "expendable" in the next push. Never, before or since, were there such generals.

The fifth revolution—the Mechanical—occurred toward the end of World War I, when the tank and the airplane made their appearance. The Mechanical Revolution, in effect, welded the firearm onto the internal combustion engine, and in so doing conferred a greater velocity and destructiveness upon Modern Warfare. By the use of internal combustion engines, either to attack the enemy or to transport troops and supplies, World War II became an amazingly fluid war of movement, so that, surpassing even its predecessor, it was able to engulf even more of the globe.

Almost at its outset, World War II also was distinguished by the sixth revolution: the Scientific. This was a literal "battle of the drawing boards" by which opposing scientists competed to supply their armies with superior weapons. If one side produced a faster, heavier tank, the other might try to counter by devising a better antitank shell. Thus, few if any campaigns in World War II ended with the same weapons with which they began. Marines who landed at Guadalcanal in August, 1942, carried the Springfield '03 rifle of World War I vintage and jumped over the side of a wooden Higgins boat, but when they left four months later it was with an M-1 semi-automatic rifle and by walking up the ramp of a steel landing craft. Thus the Scientific Revolution, which eventually was crowned by development of the atomic bomb.

It was this very advent of the Nuclear Age which introduced the seventh and last revolution: the Subversive. Because the horror of nuclear holocaust caused the men of our time to draw back from total war just as the men of the seventeenth century recoiled from it after the Thirty Years' War, Modern Warfare became limited again, and the first demonstration of this change was in the Korean War. However, the return to limited war did not mean an end to mass war or to the device of the draft. It meant only that the ultimate total weapons which might destroy mankind itself probably were not going to be used, and that in a world divided into roughly two camps —the Communist or "closed" society, and the Free or "open" society—neither side would seek the destruction of the other by force of arms.

Therefore, the seventh or Subversive Revolution introduced the era of "little wars." This is the means by which Communism, and especially Asian or Chinese Communism, seeks to control the world. Under the umbrella of nuclear forbearance, they hope to gain the allegiance of the peoples of Africa, Asia and Latin America, by far the greater part of the world's population, and thus isolate or surround the peoples of Western Europe and North America. To gain this allegiance, they have begun subversive warfare in those backward areas of the world in which the technique is most successful, and we have sought to thwart them by employing the techniques of what is called "counter-insurgency." This, of course, is what happened in Vietnam.

Subversive warfare is the attempt to negate the free world's scientific superiority by a lavish expenditure of that human life and labor in which Asia is so superabundant. Thus, it cultivates the arts of propaganda and agitation, of camouflage and cover, in a guerrilla war coldly predicated on the likelihood of an adverse casualty rate as high as 10 to 1. Under the heading of propaganda, Communist cadres infiltrate a genuine nationalist movement, such as the one begun in Vietnam, to subvert it to the Communist cause. Under agitation, the native population is taught to curse "the American imperialists" for every local calamity, while transferring to the United States a heritage of hatred for the departed colonizers of Europe. Thus, if and when the Americans do appear, they are not only at the disadvantage of seeming to oppose some genuinely nationalist movement; they are also the sort of liberators whose very looks and language make them more unpopular with the South Vietnamese than those Viet Cong and North Vietnamese who, although the enemy, are still their own countrymen. Therefore, for Americans to search for the Communist enemy in Vietnam is very much like looking for teardrops in a barrel of water; while the Americans are conversely very much like fish in the same barrel. With some exceptions being made for the Negroes or Americans of Latin blood in the armed forces, the same might be said for "wars of national liberation" fought in Africa or Latin America. This, of course, is the *sine qua non* of successful guerrilla warfare: that the enemy should be drowned in hostility. As the Communist Chinese leader Chu Teh remarked: "The guerrilla is the fish, the peasant is the water in which he swims." In its essence, therefore, subversive warfare is nothing less than a war to gain the allegiance of the native population.

This, then, is the most recent revolution to overtake Modern Warfare since the era began with the Firearms Revolution three and a half centuries ago. In all, there have been seven: Firearms, Democratic, Industrial, Managerial, Mechanical, Scientific and Subversive. Of them all, the Democratic remains the most momentous; for even the "little wars" of today are fought with the huge conscript armies made possible by the *levée en masse*. In the final analysis, the mass-man made mass-war possible. The other revolutions merely made it more horrible, or efficient, or destructive or frustrating, as the case might be. Therefore, it may be suggested that the era of Modern Warfare actually began with democracy rather than with firearms. Rousseau and his *Rights of Man* seems to have been a more powerful force than Black Berthold and his cooking pots. And this, once again, is only because it is in the heart which hates, not in the head which invents or the hand which strikes, that we find the root of war. If there had been no Firearms Revolution and no ensuing acceleration of technological progress, the Democratic Revolution still would have given birth to mass-man and hence to mass-armies. The ideals of Liberty, Equality and Fraternity have seemed even nobler than those of Faith, Hope and Charity; and Man himself, that is to say Man transfigured and deified, more worth killing for than God Himself. Whether or not it was to be done with fists or swords or rifles does not seem particularly important, for when the Common Man marched en masse to the call of bugles, "Demos rose a Demon, shriek'd and slaked the light with blood."

2. THE LARGE AND THE SMALL OF IT

At the outset of this book it was suggested that, at least in this country, war and warfare were not considered subjects worthy of study. One explanation of this might come from that befuddling, obfuscating "fog of war" that seems to rise from the pages of military history itself. It is as though many military writers consider clarity a kind of heresy, a sin to be avoided at every point where one may use some phrase from "military jargon" rather than one from ordinary speech. Probably it was inevitable that the military art, like any other calling, should develop a nomenclature or "inside" language of its own; yet, one suspects that many a military historian sometimes throws out phrases such as "double envelopment" or "flank march" chiefly because his desire, like that of a doctor saying "carcinoma" rather than "cancer" or a lawyer speaking of a "fiduciary" instead of a "trustee," is to impress his colleagues with his own credentials while appearing before the layman as one of the chosen initiates into a special branch of knowledge which is generally inaccessible (and probably also unknowable) to men of more common clay. But the fact is that military history, like anything else, can be made easy to follow once you understand the "lingo."

To begin: strategy and tactics. These two encompass all war; they are nothing but the conception and execution which are the characteristic features of any contest. Strategy conceives of how best the enemy may be overcome, tactics is the means by which this design is carried out. Strategy plans and prepares for campaigns and battles, tactics fights them.

For instance, the American strategy in the Pacific was known as "island-hopping." This plan was to avoid an island-by-island battle to break down Japan's chain of sea fortresses in the way the Japanese hoped we would do, but rather to seize only the most important islands, bypassing the rest. The tactics used to execute this concept were first to knock out enemy sea and air power in the vicinity of the target, next to bombard the island with our own air and sea power, and then to put ashore forces of landing troops to overcome the enemy garrison. Once the island was captured, it became the newest forward base for the next leapfrogging assault, while the bypassed and enemy-held islands to its rear either were neutralized by aerial bombardment or left "to wither on the vine." In this way, America was able to concentrate her full strength against only a fraction of the Japanese strength deployed to repulse her. It also obviated Japan's own strategy: to compel the United States to fight a long war so wearying and so costly that she would agree to negotiate a peace favorable to Japan. Japan's strategy was faulty in two respects, however: first, she underestimated the American fighting capacity; second, she overestimated her own resources.

Strategy, therefore, should always be based on a true estimate of one's resources; that is, the capacity to execute the design. Our own resources in World War II proved so great that we were able to exceed the Allied "grand strategy" of concentrating first against Hitler in Europe before turning to finish off Japan. This concept ordained that Japan was only to be "contained," that is, held in place and prevented from making further conquest. However, Allied resources, i.e., American, were so great that, even though Europe remained the primary theater, we were able also to exert such pressure upon Japan that she was actually ready to collapse only a few months after Germany did.

From this it may be seen that "strategy" may exist on two or more levels. For the lesser level of the Pacific there was the island-hopping or "steppingstone" strategy; for the higher one of the entire war there was the "Hitler-first" concept. Oddly enough, up until June, 1941, Hitlerite Germany does not seem to have had any formal strategy. She seems to have been swept along by events, impelled by the heady wine of victory and Hitler's faith in his destiny. If the Axis had any objective in Europe at all it would seem to have been the defeat of Britain. Britain was what Clausewitz calls "the center of gravity." Roughly, that may be interpreted to mean "strong point." Thus, a center of gravity may be a city or a river which an army seeks to hold at all costs, it may be a critical point in his line or it may be the strongest country among a coalition of powers, as Britain was the leader of the World War II Allies until America's entry.

In 1939–40, however, Hitler destroyed all the Allies but the strong one, Britain. He seemed to have thought so little of the necessity of striking at this center of gravity that he had made no preparations to invade Britain after the fall of France. Then, after he lost the aerial Battle of Britain, he turned away to attack Russia! This colossal blunder, this assault upon the Russian bear while the British bulldog was still hanging on and calling to the American giant for help, is generally considered a mistake second in magnitude only to the Japanese attack upon Pearl Harbor. It occurred, it would seem, because Hitler had no clear concept of what he wanted; no points in time and space at which he would simply stop to digest his conquests. Ironically, when he became fully embarked upon this senseless victory-bent career, he gave his opponents a clearly definable objective: himself.

Sometimes, when the makers of strategy come to select when, where and against whom they will concentrate, they depend upon factors which also govern tactics. For instance, the advantage of "interior lines" as opposed to the disadvantage of "exterior lines" influences both considerations. At present, the enemy in Vietnam is operating on strategic interior lines because he is close to his source of supply in China and the Soviet Union while we and our allies, far away from our source in the United States, are on exterior lines. Tactically, that is to say in actual battle, interior lines favor the defensive. Thus, during the Battle of Pusan in the early days of the Korean War, the United Nations forces were able to move more quickly from point to point because they were operating inside a perimeter, while the North Koreans were attacking on the outside, around the arc.

To simplify, if you were to imagine yourself in a circular position marked like a clock, you will see how you, on the interior, can move directly down from twelve o'clock to six o'clock in half the time it would take the enemy to make the same movement around the clock's outer rim. Of course, interior lines can be a distinct disadvantage in the face of superior artillery. Obviously, artillery massed around the greater extent of the outer arc can bring a greater converging fire to bear on any point within the circle. Because of this, the besiegers in the old days of limited warfare usually held the edge over the besieged. However, interior lines are generally an advantage, both tactically and strategically. No one used them better than Robert E. Lee, one of the world's masters of defensive fighting. Retreating before Grant in the Wilderness Campaign, he so cleverly fortified an inverted V position on the North Anna River that he was able to move his troops swiftly from face to face of the V, while Grant, if he desired to do the same, would be compelled to cross the river twice. Needless to say, Grant refused to be so outrageously duped.

In combination, strategy and tactics may be quite varied. The Israeli-Arab War of June, 1967 was, from the Israeli viewpoint, defensive in strategy and offensive in tactics. Believing her very existence threatened by the Arab build-up, Israel struck the first blows to defend herself. On the other hand, when Robert E. Lee invaded Pennsylvania in 1863 he was on the offensive both strategically and tactically—

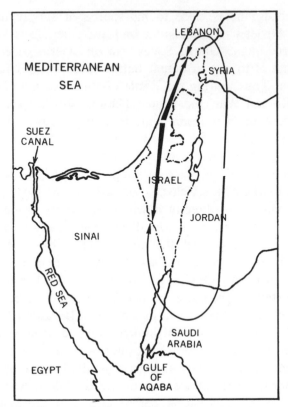

The state of Israel, apparently surrounded by her Arab enemies, presents a
striking illustration of the value of "interior lines." Except for her seaward
flank on the Mediterranean, Israel is able to move her forces from point to
point within her perimeter, that is, from foe to foe, much faster than her enemies
are able to travel around it.

strategically because he sought to draw the Federals away
from Richmond and to gain a victory that would influence
the Northern peace movement; tactically because he sought
to attack the Union's General Meade in decisive battle. However, Lee's lieutenant, James Longstreet, counseled him to
base his strategic offensive on a tactical defense; which is to
say, only to take up a position menacing Washington and
thus induce Meade to attack him. Lee refused, and there then

ensued the famous Battle of Gettysburg which military historians describe as a "meeting engagement." This is to say
that both armies were on the march and they met as though
by accident. The Confederates were actually out looking for
shoes when they ran into Federal outposts. Thereafter, more
and more units were drawn into the fight, Lee and Meade took
up positions, built up their forces—and the battle was on.

Again to differentiate between what is strategic and what
is tactical: when both concepts employ the same maneuver,
that maneuver seems to become either strategic or tactical in
exact proportion to the size or scope of the intended result.
Consider a feint. It is a threat intended to make your opponent
defend at the wrong point and thus weaken his defense where
you intend to strike. Douglas MacArthur was a great feinter,
a superb military boxer. He never feinted better than against
the Japanese on his return to Luzon. First he threatened the
southern coast, forcing the enemy to rush down there; after
which he landed in the vacated north, and after the Japanese
wheeled to repulse him there, he *did* land in the south. In
this way, he took the Japanese between two fires. Now, was
this double-feint tactical or strategic? I would say tactical,
because, even though it was done with great masses of ships
and men, it was employed to win only one of many Pacific
campaigns, not the entire war.

A true strategic feint, one that might have won an entire
continent, might have occurred in Korea. This time, it was
MacArthur who might have taken the bait; for it was he who
argued that the United States should commit itself there to an
all-out war against Communism. The Truman administration,
however, believed that Joseph Stalin was trying to embroil us
in a hopeless war with the Chinese Communists and their
North Korean allies, thus drawing our strength away from
Europe and leaving it naked to Soviet ambition there. If such
a feint had truly been intended, it would have been strategic
in the most overwhelming sense.

From MacArthur again comes a splendid example of how

a simple tactical maneuver, employed on a grand scale, can be genuinely strategic. This is the "turning movement" or "deep envelopment." Because the phrase "turning movement" is sometimes confused with a flanking attack which "turns" either extremity of the enemy's line, it will be perhaps clearer to use the term "deep envelopment." This is the maneuver by which one general strikes deep in his opponent's rear, compelling him to "turn" to confront this new danger. The depth of the thrust is of capital importance. For instance, at the Battle of Long Island in the Revolution, Sir William Howe, a fine tactician, successfully turned Washington's left flank or side and got into his rear. He did not, however, destroy the American, chiefly because the envelopment was not "deep" enough. He did not get so far behind Washington that he was able to cut him off from his base and thus force him to turn around.

A deep envelopment generally envisions the destruction of the enemy by severance of his supply line. Invading armies almost always depend on lines of supply and communications extending back to their home base. Invaders are *sometimes* able to live off the land, as Napoleon's French did in Italy in the campaigns of 1796–97; but a modern army fights with oil and ammunition, and these are vital supplies which can hardly be requisitioned from the countryside. A modern army at the end of its supply line is much like an army of termites at the end of the mud tunnel connecting them with their life-giving earth.

In Korea in the summer of 1950, even as the Communists pushed the UN Command into its last-ditch defensive perimeter at Pusan, Douglas MacArthur devised an amphibious landing at Inchon, on the west coast of the peninsula, 250 miles deep in the enemy's rear. While the Reds hammered in futility at the Pusan gate, MacArthur swung another door shut behind them at Inchon. He cut their supply line and took up blocking positions along their escape routes. When the North Koreans learned of this, they disengaged at Pusan, "turned" and fled for home. As they did the Americans and their allies in the South broke out in pursuit. The landing force at Inchon thus became the anvil on which the Pusan hammer broke the North Korean Army. By this single daring and splendid stroke, MacArthur ended the war between North and South Korea. The Communist Chinese later intervened to start a brand new war, but as far as military history goes, MacArthur's deep envelopment was a strategic stroke of the highest order: it shattered the North Korean Army.

Lord Howe's envelopment of Washington's left flank at Long Island was a tactical movement because it was limited in concept, and resulted in his winning only one battle, that is to say, a temporary advantage. MacArthur's was strategic because it was deep and decisive, winning a war. From these two operations, then, it should be possible to discern the difference between strategy and tactics.

3. CHOOSE YOUR WEAPONS

If there is one thing certain about warfare it is that it is uncertain and constantly changing. The purposes of war—the objectives—may remain fairly constant and easily defined. But the means of winning, the tactics, are forever changing—and this is probably because they are adapted to the shifting, variable factors of terrain, weapons, weather and men.

Terrain is especially decisive in one's choice of tactics. The blitzkrieg or lightning-war tactics which Hitler used to overrun France in 1940, and with which the Israelis defeated the Arabs in 1967, could never be employed in the rugged mountains of Korea or in the river-laced forests of rural Vietnam. The level terrain of northern France was ideal for fast-moving mechanized troops and tanks supported by aircraft. So were the sands of the Sinai and the Jordanian plain, especially after the Israelis destroyed the Arab airpower. In 1944 also, George S. Patton, Jr., the swashbuckling commander of armor whom Hitler called "that crazy cowboy general," sent his tanks and troop carriers clanking across France in a spectacular dash; but in the previous year the same general and the same armor were slowed to a crawl in the mountainous terrain of Sicily.

Korea's mud and hills likewise immobilized American armor. Actually, the Korean terrain compelled both sides to return to the static "position warfare" of World War I. In the years 1951–53, both sides constructed elaborate trench-and-bunker systems from which they struck at each other with artillery, sent out patrols and sometimes launched mass attacks, even as it had been done in 1914–18. Vietnam, of course, or at least the areas in which the war is being fought, is so densely overgrown and its very earth (especially during the monsoons) so moist and yielding that armored warfare there usually is no more possible than a slugging match in quicksand. True, there are large stretches of open country suitable for armored maneuver, but so far the enemy has chosen to stay out of the open, so that Vietnam is the guerrilla war par excellence, a veritable war without fronts. Thus, the rapid striking power peculiar to the blitzkrieg is of no use: i.e., there is nothing either to penetrate or to turn. Terrain, then, is of powerful importance when choosing one's tactics; as the road-bound, technocratic French discovered when they unsuccessfully sought to overwhelm the will-of-the-wisp Vietminh with the weapons and tactics of World War II.

If one examines terrain from the standpoint of geography, it may be seen how controlling this factor can be in a country's military history. Probably, the location of Germany between the two great powers of France and Russia has had as much to do with German militance as the Prussian spirit of militarism. Conversely, Swiss neutrality is possible chiefly because no one as yet has found a use and hence a desire for all those mountaintops. Belgium could not preserve her neutrality, nor could her allies guarantee it, simply because her level terrain and proximity to France make her the ideal invasion route to Paris. Proximity, incidentally, makes more for war than for peace. We have invaded Canada twice and Mexico once, and it may be observed that Anglo-French amity dates only from the Crimean War, that is to say, a little more than a century ago, but their enmity stretches back nine centuries to 1066. Unless the Cold War confrontation occasions some radical change in foreign policy, it is likely that we will continue to have unruffled relations with the Melanesians of New Guinea.

In another way, terrain can be used tactically, either as the swamp or river on which one anchors one's flank, as a height commanding the enemy's advance, or even, as with the Russians facing Napoleon in 1812 and those resisting Hitler in 1941–42, as a "scorched earth" by which an invader is left to feed on ashes. Weather also had much to do with these last two examples, for even modern armies can be frozen by extremely cold climates. This was especially true in the high North Korean plateau. There, during their breakout from the Chinese trap at Chosin Reservoir, the American Marines were compelled to run the engines of their vehicles every hour to keep them from freezing. There, where the iron earth was often too hard to dig foxholes, barricades could be made of frozen bodies; and men often freed their frozen rifle bolts by urinating on them. Extreme heat has the opposite effects, so that armies must prepare to treat victims of heat exhaustion rather than frostbite, and to place almost as much emphasis on maintaining supplies of water as on stocks of ammunition. Weather will also control an army's choice of weapons. Obviously, the sort of quick-firing gun which operates smoothly in moderate or hot climates will falter and perhaps freeze in cold ones.

Weapons themselves are the third cause of the changing character of tactics. For example, if one man is armed with a pistol and another with a rifle, it is likely that the rifleman would prefer the defensive where his superior range gave him the advantage, and the pistolman would adopt the tactics of the surprise attack. To reduce the rifleman's range superiority, the pistolman would attempt to steal as close to him as possible before opening fire. He would probably also prefer to attack under cover of night or from some unlikely point, hoping to get "in close" where his shorter weapon would be easier to wield and the rifle would be clumsy. The pistol, then, almost compels an attack, while the rifle seems to favor the defense. Changing the analogy to knife and rifle it will be seen how the surprise attack is even of so much more importance to the holder of the knife. If both opponents are armed with knives, then both will seek to close, and the contest will probably be short and to the death. If both hold rifles, both will probably take cover and bang away at each other from long range, with the likelihood that one or both will make off during the night.

In the Pacific War, the Japanese were similar to the man with the pistol. Their weapons were inferior to ours. Also, they had a naive belief that their "spiritual power," i.e., their supposedly greater courage, was superior to our firepower. So they attacked at night en masse, coming at a screaming run in hopes of closing with the bayonet. This was the famous "banzai charge" which was always broken in blood. Gradually, the Americans adjusted their own tactics to meet it, digging in a few hours before nightfall on the day of the landing, throwing up barbed wire, "zeroing-in" mortars and artillery and arranging for warships offshore to support them with naval gunfire as well as to fire flares to light the battlefield. Eventually, thoughtful Japanese came to deride these suicidal charges as "bamboo spear tactics," developing a doctrine of "defense in depth" which made the last stages of the Pacific War the bloodiest. Defense in depth is exactly what it sounds like, an area fortified and garrisoned point-to-point, rather than a single encircling cordon which can easily be broken. Each point being mutually supporting, the task of reducing one or the other must always be undertaken under fire. These were the defensive tactics used at Peleliu and Iwo Jima, the two most frightful battles of the Pacific War.

Terrain evidently has a major influence on one's choice of weapons. In level ground or rolling countryside long-range weapons of high accuracy are superior, therefore favoring the defensive. To understand this, one need only stand on Seminary Ridge where the Confederates massed for Pickett's charge against the Federals on Cemetery Ridge a clear, green, rolling mile away; and understanding it, one cannot but wonder why that suicidal charge ever was allowed to go forward. In terrain suitable to the tactics of surprise and ambush, short-range, automatic weapons are best. This is true of street fighting and jungle warfare.

A soldier's very physical characteristics have much to do with weapon design. In Vietnam, the Americans have made good use of the M-16 automatic rifle, finally correcting its tendency to jam by chrome-plating the receiver and providing it with a heavier barrel. Yet, formidable as the M-16 might be in the hands of the "Grunts," it is not quite so effective when carried by the South Vietnamese or our other Asian allies. This is because they are smaller than we are, and the M-16, as well as the M-14 or M-1, is simply too heavy for him. If he puts an M-1 to his shoulder he has trouble reaching the trigger; if he puts it under his armpit it kicks him in the nose. He needs, therefore, a lighter, shorter weapon with much the same firepower. But to devise and issue this is likely to complicate the logistics problem further, inasmuch as there will then be two types of shoulder weapon requiring two types of ammunition. Send the wrong type to the wrong unit, and you will have another costly battlefield mixup.

The fourth factor controlling one's choice of tactics is the character and habits of the enemy himself. If he is bold, you will be wary; if he is timid, you will intimidate; if he is cautious, you will be daring; if he is thorough, you will be careful; and where he hesitates, you will strike: for the conservative man can be bluffed, the overconfident one surprised, the lazy overwhelmed and the slow outdistanced.

Knowledge of one's enemy must by all means include insight into the fighting quality of his troops. In World War II, for example, General Eisenhower needed to reduce the island stronghold of Pantellaria before invading Sicily. Convinced that Pantellaria's troops "had had a stomachful of war and were looking for any good excuse to quit," Ike subjected the island to six days and nights of aerial bombardment with the result that the garrison, safe and snug in bomb shelters and barely scratched, actually did surrender without a fight. In Korea, the Communist Chinese customarily probed the United Nations line in search of those South Korean units for which they had great contempt. Conversely, the Red Chinese had so much respect for the American Marines who had used them so badly during the breakout from Chosin that they never afterward attacked them in front.

On the individual level, and again in Korea, General Matthew Ridgway shrewdly guessed that his opponent holding Seoul was timid, so he deliberately began a flanking movement designed to "aim a threat against the mind of the enemy commander" and so bluffed him into evacuating the South Korean capital. Alexander did much the same with King Darius of Persia, 2,300 years ago at Arbela, the battle that decided the fate of Asia. Alexander boldly led an attack on the person of the Persian king, so unnerving Darius that he fled the field to present Alexander the victory which crushed Persia.

One of the distinguishing features of our own Civil War was the intensely personal conflict between the rival generals. Almost all of the ranking commanders had either been to West Point together or had served with one another in the Mexican War. They knew each other's strengths and weaknesses, and they acted upon them. Joe Johnston of the South defended Richmond by dazzling George McClellan with a display of dummy cannon and troops marching and countermarching to simulate great numbers, and McClellan hesitated long enough for Johnston to fall back on the Confederate capital. McClellan, incidentally, was one of those "bloodless" generals who appear and reappear in history, full of the highest skill and the deepest compassion, promising that brains, not blood, will win the battle. Yet a battlefield without blood is as likely as a forest without leaves, and the truth about bloodless generals seems to be that they are pretenders flinching from the cruel necessity of ordering men to their deaths. As Clausewitz said: "Let us not hear of generals who conquer without bloodshed. If a bloody slaughter is a horrible sight, then that is a ground for paying more respect to war . . ."

Robert E. Lee also fought his battles with a hand on his enemy's pulse. He seems to have suspected that "Fighting Joe" Hooker of the Union was one of those generals who never retreat until the first shot is fired. At any rate, he took an awful chance in front of Hooker at Chancellorsville when he held his position in front of him with a mere handful, holding the Northern general in place while Stonewall Jackson went marching wide around Hooker's right to turn and deliver the "flanking attack" that routed him. Here, by the way, is that aforementioned "flank march." It is to move across the enemy's front in order to get at his flank, and it is a very dangerous maneuver if only because you risk being hit while you are strung out on the march.

Knowing your enemy (and yourself) was also one of U. S. Grant's cardinal rules of war. He thought so little of Gideon Pillow at Fort Donelson that he wrote in contempt: "I had known General Pillow in Mexico, and judged that with any force, no matter how small, I could march up to within gunshot of any entrenchments he was given to hold." He did, too, and was able to compel Fort Donelson to make the unconditional surrender which fitted Grant's initials and made him famous. U. S. Grant, however, had no such contempt for Lee, which is why he fought his Wilderness Campaign with the tactics of sideslipping left, sideslipping left, always trying to get around "Marse Robert's" right or to lure him out of his entrenchments.

If the factors of terrain, weapons, weather and men are decisive in the formulation of tactics, the commanders who choose them are not always inerrant in their selection. One reason for this seems to be that, in the beginning at least, new wars are always being fought with the tactics of the old. Another is that the victor never seems to question methods which once served him well, while the vanquished is anxious to find out what went wrong. Thus, after World War I, the French and British were satisfied to depend upon tactics which were in the main the same defensive ones which had triumphed in trench warfare. The Germans, dissastisfied, looked around for something different and came up with the blitzkrieg theories advanced, not by their own officers, but by such neglected or derided Allied theorists as J. F. C. Fuller and Liddell Hart in Britain and in France a man named Charles de Gaulle. A contented general, then, would seem to be as much a contradiction in terms as a "bloodless" one; and in this context one can positively *see* Joe Hooker examining his fortifications and murmuring, "How strong! How strong!" just before Lee left-hooked him across the Rapidan. By definition, preparation for war or a battle should be a calculation of probabilities, and when tactics misfire it is only because of miscalculation of one or another of these factors of terrain, weapons, weather or enemy.

Tactics, of course, need not always be those of violence. Guile and gold, so efficacious in peace, are equally fruitful in war. In Biblical times, Jericho was probably betrayed to Joshua by the harlot Rahab; and it is possible that when Quebec fell to James Wolfe in 1759, his secret path ascending to the Plains of Abraham might have been picked out for him by corrupt French officials seeking the ruin of the colony so that all record of their thievery might also be destroyed. British gold made a traitor of Benedict Arnold (on his own initiative, of course), and it also secured the services of Marshal Tito's anti-Hitlerite partisans in World War II, although it could not buy Tito or keep Yugoslavia from going Communist once the war was over.

Of all the ruses of warfare, the device of the Trojan horse still seems to stand supreme in history; although it probably did not happen exactly as Vergil describes it. Look at this preposterous proposition! Early one morning the Trojans peer out from their beleaguered city to see that the Greeks have vanished. After ten bloody years during which the great sprawling military camp has been thrown up on the plain before Troy, the Greeks have overnight wrapped up the entire business in a napkin, taken ship and sailed away. In their place stands this huge wooden horse. Did the Greeks throw it up overnight? Did they use silent hammers? Even if they did, what would the Trojans want with a wooden horse, anyway? Yet, the legend tells us that these obliging Trojans trundled it inside their heretofore invincible city, only to discover with some surprise that the Greeks were not gone at all but *inside the horse*.

So goes Vergil's charming story. In fairness to him, however, it should be made clear that he did not offer his *Aeneid* as pure history but only as an epic based on legends. There appears no doubt that Troy was undone by guile, but probably not by so crude and palpable a stratagem as the wooden horse. There are any number of probabilities, not excepting the likelihood that the so-called "horse" actually may have been one of those wooden towers which besiegers in the age of Historic Warfare used to drag up to a city's walls so that soldiers might mount them to pour flights of arrows, showers of stones or vessels of flaming oil into the streets below. Nor can we rule out a "fifth column" such as the presence of a "Greek party" in Troy—to say nothing of the possible growth, after so many trying years, of a considerable Trojan peace movement—or even the possibility that the Greeks finally got to some gatekeeper and crossed his palm with silver. Nevertheless, many a city has been taken by a ruse; and a far likelier as well as more ingenious trick seems to have been employed by Genghis Khan against the Chinese city of Volohai in the thirteenth century. Unable to take his fortress by storm, the Khakan ordered his men to trap all the cats and swallows in the vicinity. Next he commanded them to tie tufts of cottonwool to the tails of the beasts, and then to light the tufts and turn both cats and swallows loose. At once the terrified swallows rose into the air and flew for their nests in the city, while the enraged cats sped home for their lairs. A few of them perished enroute, a few were killed by the citizens of Volohai, but most got home and set the city blazing in a thousand places. While the inhabitants were busy fighting fires, Genghis Khan and his warriors entered their city.

Perhaps the greatest of ruses, or at least one which must stand as unique for its sheer subtlety and insight into human nature, was devised by Alexander, the greatest of captains. In his Balkan and Illyrian campaign of 335 B.C., Alexander's problem was how to draw Glaucias and his wild Taulantians from their secure position in the hills down into the plains where the superior discipline of Alexander's troops would defeat them. So he held a parade! Realizing that there are few events more likely to draw a crowd than a military spectacle, he ordered his cavalry and infantry to perform a battle drill. Enchanted, the Taulantians began to congregate on the lower slopes of the foothills for a closer view. When, as Arrian writes, they became absorbed by both "the smartness and the discipline of these maneuvers," Alexander gave the order to attack. Raising a terrifying cheer, clanging their spears on their shields, Alexander's infantry rushed and routed their startled audience.

Finally, there are the tactics of terror. All warrior races (including our own "peace-loving" Americans) have at one time or another resorted to deliberate slaughter and destruction in an effort to terrify or intimidate the enemy. The Assyrians, of course, the first practitioners of terrorism known to history, may have been the most exquisitely cruel; certainly their customs of skinning prisoners alive or impaling them on stakes have yet to be exceeded. They were also effective, for many a Middle Eastern city, trembling in the knowledge of what happened to those who resisted these big-nosed, curly-headed sadists, opened its gates upon the mere blast of an Assyrian trumpet. The Mongols were no less sadistic, although apparently not as purposeful: there seems to be no sense at all to Tamerlane and his tower of skulls. But Basil II of Constantinople was much more objective in his cruelty, when, to rid himself of the Bulgar nuisance on his borders, he put out the eyes of 15,000 Bulgar captives, sparing one man in every hundred to lead these pitiful battalions of the blind back to their horrified tsar.

Oliver Cromwell of England, an undoubted cavalry genius but also one of those religious fanatics who feel themselves "called" to kill and burn in the name of the Lord, was unsparing in his use of terror against the Irish. Reporting to Parliament on the bloody massacre at Drogheda, he concluded: "I wish that all honest hearts may give the glory of this to God alone, to whom indeed the praise of this mercy belongs." This "mercy" (by which the Lord High Protector probably meant "blessing") included driving people into churches and burning them alive, ripping helpless women "up the fundament" and selling all survivors who were not "knocked on the head" into slavery.

Probably because no one hates like brothers, the histories of civil wars are full of examples of the most loathesome and "unnecessary" cruelty. Once again, the French Revolution seems to be an outstanding example of unbridled passion. The unlettered peasants of the Vendée were surely guilty of the most abominable treatment of the soldiers they captured during their abortive counter-revolution; and yet, the educated "humanists" of the Convention went even further. Here is the report of a Republican general named Westermann: "I have crushed the children under the hoofs of horses, massacred the women . . . who will breed no more brigands. I have not a single prisoner with which to reproach myself. We take no prisoners; it would be necessary to feed them with the bread of Liberty." This, in the name of Liberty, Equality and Fraternity; and yet, one is almost pleased to discover that in the same name Westermann went to his own execution a year later.

In our own Civil War, William Tecumseh Sherman made the tactics of terrorism an accepted and even valued form of warfare. To his credit, "Uncle Billy" prohibited civilian bloodshed, but when he began his famous march from Atlanta to the sea it was with the avowed intention to "make Georgia howl." Sherman may have been the first commander to make deliberate war against the will of an enemy population, and when he cut his path of destruction 60 miles wide and 300 miles long, he not only struck at the soul of the South but also at the hungry belly of Lee's army in Virginia. Here, then, are the first faint lineaments of the monster of *Schrecklichkeit* or "frightfulness" which the Nazis used in France and the Low Countries. Massed bombing of cities was intended not only to terrify the civil population, but also to force a flood of refugees onto the highways where they and their vehicles might be bombed and machine-gunned and thus, by clogging the roads, make military movement impossible. The North Koreans made use of refugees in a different way: massing crowds of uprooted South Korean civilians, including women and children, they drove them before them at gunpoint to form a kind of human shield behind which their own soldiers might advance.

Obviously, the uses of terror are varied, culminating in our own time by our own use of atomic bombs to strike at an enemy population's will, and the Viet Cong's slaughter of tens of thousands of village headmen, teachers, technicians and priests in a calculated campaign against a country's brains. It would seem pointless to argue on our behalf that the impersonal atomic bombings of Hiroshima and Nagasaki "saved lives" or "shortened the war" (as they certainly did *not* do), or for the Viet Cong to maintain that their own more personal terrorism is in the interests of conferring the blessings of Communism on a backward society; what is to the point in this study is to suggest that men at all times and in all places have seldom hesitated to use the weapons and the tactics that will give them victory.

4. FUSTEST WITH THE MOSTEST

Like fashions in dress, thought and literature, there are fashions in war; and these, like the seasons, seem to be composed of four basic forms; pounce-and-withdraw, mass-and-maneuver, siege, and attrition.

It is even likely that any age characterized by a preference for one form, such as the era of Primitive Warfare's use of the tactics of pounce-and-withdraw, may also employ one or all of the other three. Thus, when men of that age laid waste their neighbor's food garden they were using the tactic of attrition which aims at wearying and exhausting the enemy. When the Communists in Vietnam employ the tactics of pounce-and-withdraw now known as guerrilla warfare, our countering tactic of search-and-destroy is also a form of attrition. Siege warfare, the means by which a city or a fortified place is either stormed or starved into submission, is a form of mass-and-maneuver in the general assault which may seek to overwhelm it, or of attrition in the encircling lines which may try to weary and exhaust it.

Similarly, the success of one form of warfare may call forth a kind of defense which will compel a change to another form. Thus, when Historic Warfare began with organized armies using the tactics of mass-and-maneuver, the victories won by this form of war caused the rise of walled or fortified cities throughout the Middle East. This in turn compelled the Assyrians to bring the arts of siege warfare to a high degree of perfection. They developed siege engines such as battering rams and assault towers and even fielded corps of pioneers

42

trained to undermine a city's walls by hacking away at its foundations under cover of wicker mantlets erected over approach trenches. When battle "opened up" again with the Persians, mobility was increased by what appears to be the first use of cavalry, probably borrowed from those savage Scythians who came galloping out of Central Asia to inspire the Greek myth of the satyr: a creature half man and half horse.

But no matter how battle is joined or under what form war is being waged, it is directed against three points of the enemy's "line": left, right and center. And every one of these three subdivisions also has its own subdivisions of a center and its two extremities, or "flanks" as they are called. A successful blow on any one of these three points is generally sufficient to disorganize and even to demoralize the enemy. If the blow is aimed at left or right, the maneuver is a "flanking attack." If it is at the center, it is a "frontal assault" usually aimed at achieving a "penetration" or "breakthrough."

Simple as this appears, it will be seen that all sorts of combinations may follow from the art of maneuvering one's troops so that one may strike the weakest point with the greatest mass. A feigned flanking attack may be followed by a frontal assault, or vice versa, or a feint at the left be succeeded by an attack upon the center and right. In rare cases, such as the final Allied offensive in World War I, it is even possible to strike at all three points, all along the line; but this unusual method can only apply to unusual circumstances, e.g., a "war without flanks" such as the stalemated Western front in 1914–18. With the opposing armies in firm position from the Alps to the sea, flanking maneuver was not possible. Normally, the idea is to concentrate at one decisive point.

Always, in Primitive, Historic or even Modern Warfare, the intent has been to employ the bulk of one's forces against a fraction of the enemy's. In the frontless war fought in Vietnam, the objective is still to get two men on one or even three on one. Even the element of surprise envisions superiority: the advantage held by ten prepared men over a hundred unprepared. In armored warfare, the trick is to get tanks against foot troops or airplanes against tanks. Always and in every place, the wise commander seeks to pit superior against inferior force. To do this, he usually also has a "reserve" stationed somewhere behind his front line. This is a body of troops purposely withheld from the opening action so that it may be employed at the critical moment, its decisive weight to be felt when the enemy is at the breaking point, or else rushed into the breach when one's own line is in danger of giving way. When your reserve is gone and things are still going badly, it is generally a good idea to start packing. The reserve, in effect, is your "last bolt." Reading Winston Churchill's *Memoirs,* one can feel the appalling sense of disaster which seized him, when, to his question, "Where is the reserve?" the French replied: "Gone." As Churchill well knew, so was France.

Center, left and right, then, are the three zones of battle, the three points of a line; and the reserve is that which may reinforce and thus participate in any one of them. No matter how tactics change or evolve, basically they are always directed toward bringing superior force to bear at any one of these points. To do this, of course, there have been corresponding changes in soldiery and military formations.

During the late, heroic period of what has here been called the age of Historic Warfare, the warriors were the nobles, the only ones who could afford a horse and chariot and the weapons of the day. Usually, a noble's poorly armed or unarmed retainers were hardly more than servitors and cheerleaders. In heroic combat, the warriors drove onto the field in their chariots, even as Achilles and Hector in Homer's great epic, hurling their light missile spears at each other, and then, failing to bring their opponents down, dismounting to pursue the fight with the sword. The bow, though already in use for hunting, at least, was scorned as a cowardly weapon unfit for heroes, and it is likely that when the baseborn shepherd youth David killed the noble champion Goliath with his cowardly slingshot, there was much grumbling about "unsportsmanlike conduct" in the camp of the Philistines. However that may be, heroic combat was a strictly personal, hand-to-hand engagement between rival champions or heroes, and it did not change until roughly the sixth or seventh century before Christ when increasing prosperity and improvements in the smelting of metal for armor and weapons put a warrior's panoply within economic reach of well-to-do commoners as well as the highborn. When this occurred, the first "new" soldier in military history appeared. He was the Greek hoplite or heavy infantryman, vested in metal helmet, breastplate, leg and thigh guards, and armed with a heavy shield, long thrusting spear and heavy sword.

Greek Hoplites

At that time, Hellas, or what is now called ancient Greece, was a cluster of city-states, each with its own walled town surrounded by outlying farms and villages. Warfare among the city-states was almost endemic; and just as it is today, those rude democracies of old compelled all free men to serve. The most well-to-do were the elite or hoplites. Although there were lighter, auxiliary troops, the hoplite was the true arbiter of battle, marching and countermarching in a tightly-packed formation called a "phalanx."

And here is as good a point as any to try to clear up the confusion often connected with the distinction to be made between a "phalanx" or a "column," "ranks" and "files" and "enfilade" and "defilade." Basically, it is all a matter of front and flank, the side-by-side or horizontal axis of a formation and the front-to-rear or vertical axis. If you were to take fifty men and form them in five left-to-right lines, one behind the other, each a few feet apart, you would have a "phalanx." This is because the formation offers the broadest front; it is ten men wide but only five men deep. But if these same men were to make a right- or left-face the same formation would be in "column." Its front or side-to-side axis would be only five men wide, but its length or front-to-rear axis would be ten men deep. A column, then, is deeper than it is wide; just as a phalanx is wider than it is deep.

The distinction between rank and file is similar. You con-

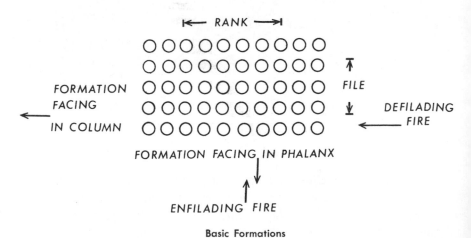

Basic Formations

sider yourself in ranks in respect to the men on either side of you, in files in relation to the men before and behind you. And when we speak of enfilade or defilade, it is once again a matter of front and flank. To take the enemy in "enfilading fire" is to fire upon his side-by-side axis, to lay down "defilading fire" is to shoot at him along the front-and-rear axis.

So the Greek hoplites fought in phalanxes, section after section of armored spearmen perhaps twenty men wide and eight men deep, each section arrayed one beside the other to make an ever broader, more bristling phalanx. This was the formation out of which Philip of Macedon created the all-conquering "Macedonian phalanx." Philip, of course, did not invent the formation; instead, he lengthened his hoplite's spear or sarissa to an eventual and incredible reach of 14 feet. Thus the spears of the soldiers in the fifth rank reached beyond the body of the soldier in the first. What a bristling iron hedgehog that Macedonian phalanx must have been, and it is no exaggeration to say that Philip's son, the great Alexander, conquered the world with "a foot and a half of iron." Alexander, of course, did not rely merely on the foot soldiers, but also on his heavy cavalry, troops of heavily armored lancers who came to be called "cataphracts." In fact, Alexander broke down the solid wall of the phalanx into separate mobile blocks, using the entire formation, not to crush and impale the enemy upon some invincible juggernaut of spear points, but rather like a mobile fortress from behind which he might mass and hurl his decisive arm, his cavalry.

However, as Lynn Montross has so aptly observed, "It is always some conception of the human wall that is the beginning and end of all tactics." Thus, as the decadent Greeks after Alexander relapsed into ever more solid phalanxes as a kind of sanctuary, the emerging and adventurous Romans broke theirs down into ever more separate and more maneuverable blocks. In the end, they developed the little phalanx of 120 men called the maniple. These maniples were formed into cohorts or battalions of 420 men composed of three 120-man maniples of young and veteran troops and one 60-man maniple of older reserves. Ten cohorts made the famous Roman legion of 4,200 foot soldiers which, with 300 attached cavalry, totaled 4,500 men.

Because of the maniple, the Roman battle line was an extraordinarily fluid formation. It was as supple and adroit as the human hand; our very word "manipulate" derives from it. Ordinarily, the Roman legion formed in three lines 250 feet apart. The first line was composed of ten maniples each occupying a front 60 feet wide and 45 feet deep, and each spaced one maniple-front away from each other. The second line was formed the same way, except that its maniples were drawn up behind the intervals of the first line, checkerboard fashion. Thus, if hard pressed, the first line might retreat into the intervals of the second; or, if needed, the second line could advance into the intervals of the first. Meanwhile, a third line of ten 60-man and ten 120-man maniples formed a reserve.

As it evolved, the Roman legion came to depend upon two weapons: the pilum, a seven-foot throwing and thrusting spear; and the *gladius,* the famous short sword twenty inches long with a thick, four-inch-wide, double-edged blade. Hurled from short distances, the pilum could pierce the heaviest armor; and the *gladius* could cut off a man's arm or leg at a blow. There were, of course, lighter weapons such as javelins, as well as heavier, special engines of war for sieges. In the main, however, 3,000 of the legion's 4,200 foot soldiers carried the pilum and the *gladius.*

It was with this formation and these weapons that Rome

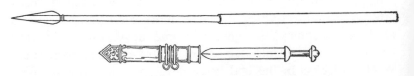

Roman Pilum and Gladius

conquered; perhaps still more by the awesome discipline of her battle line. No militant nation before or since has understood human psychology better than Rome. She knew well that most men would rather flee than fight. That was why she evolved that consummate battle line marked by the spirit of comradeship, where every mind was merged into one. Compelled to confront great gatherings of barbarians, she countered superiority of numbers with strength of will. Her lines stood still and unflinching before the onslaught of the mob. At a command, the front could be doubled and made formidable as a wall; at another, it could fall back 250 feet and be another wall. Ultimately, Roman discipline exhausted the barbarians until the swarm's courage melted away and the feeling of mob-bravery gave way to that of mob-panic.

And yet, great as Rome was militarily, the most famous battle of all time is associated with one of her greatest defeats. This was on the plain of Cannae in Italy in the year 216 B.C., at the hands of Hannibal, the great captain of Carthage. Although most major victories are as much due to accident as design, Hannibal seems deliberately to have planned to trap the Roman army under Caius Terentius Varro in a monster ambush. He drew up his lines with his wings straight but his center extended outward in convex form. Hannibal's intent was to allow the Romans to push the convex center inward, to drive it backward into a concave form—and at that instant to swing his wings forward and so surround the entire Roman army. This is exactly what happened, and of Varro's force of 85,000 men only 15,000 survived. Cannae has since become the model of the perfect victory, that "double envelopment" by which the enemy is encircled either to be slaughtered or captured. To understand the term better, one may imagine a wrestler getting one arm around his opponent, and thus "enveloping" him; if he gets both arms around his opponent he has "doubly enveloped" him.

This is what Hannibal did, and yet, unrivaled as his victory remains, it was in the end no more than a mere tactical advantage. Hannibal, it appears, comprehended battle but not war. "You know how to win victories," a lieutenant said to him on the morrow of Cannae, "but not how to use them." Cannae only compelled Rome to fall back upon her greatness, to rally and resist, to draw upon her superior resources, and to win, nine years later, the less spectacular but strategically decisive victory of the Metaurus River.

That battle, incidentally, is a striking illustration of the

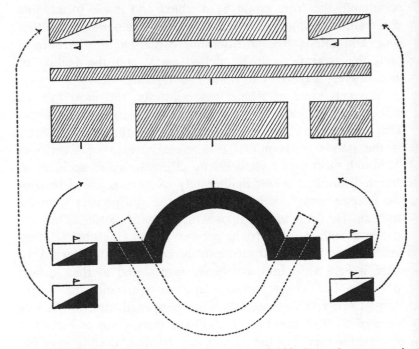

At Cannae, Hannibal arrayed his Carthaginians (solid black) in what appeared to be a great human arc, with his cavalry and light infantry on the wings. The Romans (shaded lines) attacked directly against the Carthaginian convex center, pushing it back into a concave formation (dotted line). After the Roman wings followed the center into the trap, Hannibal's infantry wings and light horse closed in on the Roman flanks, surrounding them. Hannibal's heavy horse, meanwhile, fell on the Roman rear to complete the slaughter. Cannae remains the classic example of "double envelopment."

value of "interior lines," showing how a commander lying
between two enemy armies may attack one before the other
can come to the rescue, and then, if he wishes, wheel to destroy
the second. At the time, Hannibal's brother, Hasdrubal, was
advancing from Spain into Italy. He sought to join Hannibal,
a fusing of forces that could have been ruinous to Rome. However, Claudius Nero, the Roman commander facing Hannibal
at Apulia, learned of Hasdrubal's intentions. At once he left
his main body facing Hannibal, and with a picked force of
about 7,000 men made a forced march to the north to reinforce Livius opposite Hasdrubal at the Metaurus. There, at
a council of war, he urged an immediate attack. As is usual
in a council of war, the more numerous fainthearts gained the
upper hand, and one officer argued for a delay, suggesting that
Nero's exhausted men needed time to rest from their march.
Nero's reply is worth quoting: "The officer who is for giving
time to my men here to rest themselves, is for giving time to
Hannibal to attack my men whom I have left in the camp in
Apulia. He is for giving time to Hannibal and Hasdrubal to
discover my march, and to maneuver for a junction with each
other in Cisalpine Gaul at their leisure. We must fight instantly, while both the foe here and the foe in the south are
ignorant of our movements. We must destroy this Hasdrubal,
and I must be back in Apulia before Hannibal awakes from
his torpor."

Hasdrubal was destroyed, and Nero immediately hurried
south to toss the slain Carthaginian commander's bloody head
into Hannibal's camp at Apulia. And when that grisly message
of defeat came sailing over the ramparts, it also signaled the
doom of Carthage. Six decades later the ruthless Romans
deliberately cremated their enemy's city in fire and salt.

But Rome was also mortal, and as it began to sink into its
long, lingering decline, a vast change overtook the art of war.
Cavalry superseded infantry. The dreaded Roman legion fell
into dissolution and decay, eventually vanishing entirely from

the field. From the Metaurus in 207 B.C. to the Roman disaster at Adrianople in 378 A.D., a span of nearly six centuries, the legion had been virtually invincible. There had been an occasional military calamity, of course, particularly the defeat of Varus by the Germans under Arminius in the Teutoburger Wald in 9 A.D. Generally, however, the steady step of Roman infantry had prevailed over the wild gallop of barbarian horsemen.

But, by the middle of the third century, civil war had become endemic in the Empire. Within sixty years, no less than sixteen emperors and more than thirty would-be emperors perished in factional strife. Depleted legions or those reinforced with inferior soldiers became unable to contain the barbarian tribes pressing against such great natural barriers as the Rhine or the Danube. Although the deteriorating situation was temporarily arrested by organizers such as Diocletian and Constantine, it was never entirely retrieved. As the quality of the Imperial Army declined because of a heavy infusion of mercenaries and adventurers among the ranks of its citizen-soldiers, the prowess of mounted barbarians such as the Goths improved, probably because of three centuries of close contact with the military skill of the Empire. Barbarian weapons also improved. Concurrent with these changes, Rome found itself compelled to field more and more squadrons of cavalry. This was due to the barbarian fondness for swift, plundering raids. Heavily armored and encumbered legionaries were obviously unable to pursue and chastise mounted raiders. Horsemen were needed, even light infantry.

Nevertheless, the Imperial Army continued to rely upon its legions as the chief arbiter of battle. Then, in 378, the Emperor Valens met the Visigoths at Adrianople (Edirne in modern Turkey). It was Roman infantry against barbarian cavalry, and the mounted warriors won. Adrianople was a defeat as crushing as Cannae. Valens, most of his chief officers and 40,000 men all perished on the field. And Adrianople was certainly more significant than Cannae, for it heralded the reign of the horseman which was to endure for a thousand years.

Meanwhile, as horse gained its ascendancy over foot, tactical skill appears to have languished. Warfare became a vast swarming of mounted hordes. Generals in the Eastern Empire still cultivated the arts of war, most notably the Byzantine cavalry leader Belisarius; but in the West, battles were to be won more by hard fighting than by discipline or military skill. Gradually, with the emergence of feudalism, infantry disappeared and the true fighting man was the heavily-armored horseman fighting with shield, sword and lance. Here was the knight of old, the nobleman whose blue blood and baronial holdings were bought for him by the edge of the sword.

Between the warring worlds of Islam and Christendom, both Saracen and Frank,* as they called each other, gave battle from the saddle. The great and decisive engagement of Tours in the year 732, when Charles Martel, the grandfather of Charlemagne, turned the Mohammedan tide and sent it flowing back across the Pyrenees, seems to have been nothing more than a vast undisciplined melee between hosts of horsemen. Three and a half centuries later, when the Crusaders were the invaders, the knights who won and lost the kingdom of Jerusalem still conceived of warfare as a saddle-to-saddle struggle. So greatly was the horse esteemed that it became, in effect, the partner of the noble. The horse was "the mobile pedestal" from which the noble looked down upon the lower classes. The very first of the military and noble titles— chevalier, marshal, squire and constable—derived either from the horse itself or from the care of this "noble beast." Even today, there is not an army in the world that does not still maintain a company or two of cavalry for ceremonial purposes, and as late as 1916 a diehard cavalryman such as Sir Douglas Haig could still dream of winning great battles with cavalry charges.

In the late Middle Ages, when only the elite might ride,

* From *francisca,* the deadly German battle-ax.

the glory of battle was normally reserved for the mounted man. Footmen might serve him or even, in unusual circumstances, come to his assistance. But for footmen to *fight* was either preposterous or comical. A Frenchman describing the Battle of Senlis in 1418 wrote: "There was a captain who had a crowd of footmen who all died, and there was great laughter because they were all men of poor estate."

By then, however, the new firearms and the reappearing bow-and-arrow had both sighted in on the high-and-mighty horseman. Although guns were still crude, the bow, and especially the splendid English longbow, was a formidable weapon indeed. At Agincourt, three years before Senlis, the whistling arrows of the British bowmen cut the flower of French chivalry into bloody tatters. The actual score: 10,000 Frenchmen dead (many of them—against all the rules of war—with their throats slit because they were not worth holding to ransom) and 1,000 Frenchmen prisoners, against just 100 English dead. Almost all of the French fallen were knights, tumbled from their saddles at long range. Thus, the power of the longbow, and if the invention of gunpowder had not come so fast upon the evolution of this magnificent missile weapon, it is likely that the armies of the future would have whistled away at each other with arrows in much the same way that they were to bang away with muskets and rifles.

Even so, the feudal knight despised the bow-and-arrow as an "unfair" weapon. A "fair fight," of course, was a face-to-face encounter, but the cowardly arrow came wailing out of nowhere. Armed with such a weapon, any lowborn fellow might take the measure of his betters. Naturally enough, the gun was an even baser instrument, and by the end of the fifteenth century at least one noble was lamenting: "In olden times he received great praise and honor who let his enemy have equal arms. Challenges went out in good order to those who were good knightly people. Now no one is a good captain who cannot beat his handicapped enemy. Now he is praised and extolled in war, who is able and knows how to cheat his enemy."

Thus, as guns and bows superseded swords and lances, as the impersonal missile striking from the void supplanted the personal thrust-and-cut encounter, the foot soldier returned to battle.* Tactics became fluid again, and nowhere more than in Italy where the factional fights which embroiled city-states or ducal principalities such as Florence and Milan produced a very special kind of warfare. Here, all the fighting was done by highly-trained mercenaries hired out to the cities by their *condottieri*, or contractor captains. This was professional war par excellence and its proponents fought strictly for pay. The best *condottieri* such as Paolo Vitelli or Prospero Colonna fought for the highest bidder. As must inevitably happen when soldiers are expensive and ransom of prisoners more profitable than killing them, *condottieri* warfare was remarkably bloodless. An entire siege could be conducted with little or no loss of life. As Sir Charles Oman, the chief authority on medieval warfare, has observed:

> The consequence of leaving the conduct of war in the hands of the great mercenary captains was that it came often to be waged as a mere tactical exercise or a game of chess, the aim being to mancuvcr thc cncmy into an impossiblc situation, and thcn capture him, rather than to exhaust him by a series of costly battles. It was even suspected that condottieri, like dishonest pugilists, sometimes settled beforehand that they would draw the game. Battles when they did occur were often very bloodless affairs. . . . Machiavelli cites cases of general actions in which there were only two or three men-at-arms slain, though the prisoners were to be numbered by hundreds.

* According to Charles Hitch, author of *Decision Making for Defense,* the changes in emphasis from armored knight to bowman to musketman stemmed from changes in cost effectiveness. The bow was much cheaper than armor, could be supplied to more men and could kill armored knights from a distance. On the other hand, while the musket was not as individually effective as the bow, it was even cheaper to produce, and in the hands of still more troops could yield greater firepower.

Doubtless, *condottieri* warfare was not quite cricket; it might even have been closer to comic opera—and yet, who would not gladly return to it! Unfortunately, it was not this dainty war dance which caught the fancy of the military world, but rather the very real and very grim infantry warfare developed concurrently in Spain. At the end of the fifteenth century, the voyage of Columbus coincided with the expulsion of the last of the Moslem Moors from the Iberian Peninsula. A hardy yeomanry skilled in the use of weapons and led by proud but penniless captains, all fired by an intense nationalism and high religious zeal, as well as thirsty for gold and glory, was now available to follow in the wake of the explorers and to make Europe tremble. From the Pacific to Flanders fields they raised the battle shout of "St. James and at 'em!"—and they became the terror of the world.

Actually, the Spanish foot was the first "infantry." This was because the honorary colonels of the Spanish *tercios* or regiments were the *infantes* or princes, and the *tercios* soon came to be called *infanteria*. Borrowing some of the armor worn by the knights whom they had replaced, the Spanish were the first foot soldiers to arm themselves with a variety of weapons. In the original *tercios*, one body of troops was armed with the pike, a long wooden shaft with a pointed steel head; another with sword and buckler; and the third with crossbows and arquebus, that is, a primitive musket fired by a match and frequently supported by a forked rest. Gradually, as the pike became obsolete, more and more of the Spanish foot were armed with these matchlocks. At Pavia in 1525 the steady fire of the Spanish arquebusiers helped to win the day for Emperor Charles V over King Francis I of France, and thus Pavia is probably the first battle in which small-arms fire had a decisive effect.

Thereafter, the Spanish infantry were both the dread and the admiration of Europe, copied everywhere, until, with the advent of the Thirty Years' War, the fresh and innovating

Spanish Pikeman, Sixteenth Century

military genius of King Gustavus Adolphus of Sweden had
its effect upon infantry organization and the once-feared
Spanish Army at last went down to its death at the
Battle of Rocroy in 1643. By then, the Swedish warrior
king was dead, but his impact upon infantry tactics
was lasting. If modern warfare truly was born in the
holocaust of the Thirty Years' War, then Gustavus Adolphus
was its father. It was he who placed a new emphasis
on infantry firepower. More than the Spanish, he increased
the number of musketeers while decreasing the number of
pikemen. He also made widespread use of field artillery, that
is, guns light enough to be moved quickly by horses or men,
and organized logistics, the service of supply. Yet, if the
Protestant champion can be said to have made war more
mobile by his creation of light infantry—foot troops with less
armor and lighter weapons—it was the Catholic captain,
Albrecht von Wallenstein, who was its first true quartermaster.
Wallenstein made an exact science of logistics. His estate at
Friedland was the model of organization for war. There he

constructed factories to make munitions, mills to make flour, bakeries for bread, weaveries for clothing, breweries for beverages—and a network of roads and clearinghouses through which supplies could be carried to his troops or to huge storehouses to be held in readiness for any emergency.

Mobility, firepower and mobilization had now conspired to make war ever more frightful, and yet, even though infantry had been recrowned "Queen of Battles"—a title which it holds to this day—the actual tactics or means of winning the battles had not been altered. Basically, the captains of the Wars of Religion relied upon the power of frontal assaults. It remained for the "rosewater war" of the age of the Absolute Kings to produce Frederick the Great of Prussia and his famous "Oblique Order." Simplified, Frederick's tactics were based upon superior mobility. He believed in attacking his slower enemy's flank before he could change front. Frederick explained his tactics thus: "You refuse (i.e., bend back) one wing to the enemy and strengthen the one which is to attack. With the latter you do your utmost against one wing of the enemy, which you take in flank. An army of 100,000 men taken in flank may be beaten by 30,000 in a very short time. . . . The advantages of this arrangement are (1) a small force can engage one much stronger than itself; (2) it attacks an enemy at a decisive point; (3) if you are beaten, it is only part of your army, and you have the other three-fourths which are still fresh to cover your retreat."

Such a concept, of course, puts a very high premium on mobility, and because the Prussian king endlessly drilled his troops in the changes of front and direction necessary for his objective of rapid deployment, he has mistakenly gone into popular history as the apotheosis of the "Prussian drillmaster." Actually, this able ruler—so talented, erudite and wise that, but for his brutality and his love of conquest, he might have fulfilled Plato's prescription for the philosopher-king—considered his drill as nothing but the means to the end: success

Prussian Infantryman, ca. 1740

in battle. As Napoleon remarked, Frederick "laughed in his sleeve" at the strutting parade-ground drillmasters who mistook Frederick's drill for the art of war. They had mistaken his means of mobility for his purpose of getting quickly on his enemy's flank, and like all people guilty of this basic human tendency to confuse the end with the means, they really did not know what they were doing.

Out of this era of limited war also arose what are called "linear tactics," that is, bodies of troops formed in "lines" three ranks deep and usually firing volleys as they advanced. Surprisingly enough, these volleys were often unaimed; for the musket still seems to have been thought of as a noise and smoke-making machine which would at once terrify the enemy while providing the screen of smoke out of which the decisive bayonet charge would be launched. No commander seems to have speculated over what might have happened if these lines of brilliantly-uniformed soldiers were to advance against entrenched marksmen. Lord Howe found out at Bunker Hill, when he saw his redcoats go down in clots of crumpled scarlet and experienced "a moment that I never felt before." But the military world had yet to learn that firepower was the handmaiden of the prepared defensive; and so, as the school of attack continued in the ascendant, the bright, neatly "dressed" (straight and orderly) lines of red, blue, green or white continued to advance, firing volleys that were generally ineffective at more than forty yards' range. Doubtless, this slow and unswerving approach could be most unnerving, especially to untrained troops deployed in the open. Because of this, when the French Revolution began and most of the trained soldiery and their officers chose to fight for the Allies, it was believed that the regular armies of Europe would very easily dispose of the raw recruits of the Republic.

At Hondschoote in 1793, however, the French who suddenly scattered before the awesome advance of the allied Austrian, British and Dutch forces did not also take flight; rather, they took cover in ditches and behind hedges and began to snipe away at their frustrated enemy in much the same way that the red Indians riddled Braddock's British regulars in the French and Indian War or the American rebels hounded Gage's redcoats on the retreat from Lexington. It is likely that these French were even better shots, for most of them were poachers whose penchant for potting a few of his lordship's forbidden game had made marksmen of them. So they compelled the allied soldiery to retreat; unbroken, of course, and undefeated—but nevertheless retreating.

As battles go, Hondschoote was a trifle. But it was the birthplace of the tactics of the Revolutionary armies, the very tactics which Napoleon was to make his own. This was to take the numerous but undisciplined French and form them into columns, where they were more easily managed than in line; and next, to protect the columns with swarms of skirmishers thrown out front. Lazare Carnot, the author of the *levée en masse*, had been at Hondschoote. He had seen the effectiveness of the skirmishers. Knowing full well that undisciplined but numerous troops must needs attack, it was he, not Napoleon, who instilled this credo in the hearts of the Revolutionary generals. Carnot, then, is probably the father of democratic war. Probably he was the savior of the French Revolution as well, for it is believed to have been Carnot who awoke some six or seven thousand sleeping Frenchmen to lead them on the night march that turned the Austrian left at Wattignies. And Wattignies, a consequence of Hondschoote, was the hour of darkest peril for the Republic.

Napoleon Bonaparte, of course, the ferocious genius who eventually killed the Republic to make way for his own ephemeral Empire, was and is the greatest master of democratic war. He, too, used the column formation, probably because its mass was more suitable to furious assaults and because he preferred a penetration rather than a flanking or enveloping movement. He also frequently marched his large bodies of troops in his famous "diamond" formation; that is, four columns moving roughly equidistant from each other so that they could rapidly move to each other's assistance once a battle began. And a battle was Napoleon's chief objective: "I desire nothing so much as a big battle," he repeatedly declared, thereby violating the chief precept of the age which he was bringing to a violent end. Napoleon broke all the rules, and it seems safe to say that after him, with some exceptions concerning the treatment of prisoners, there were no more rules of war. There was one precept and one alone: success. To this end, the great but unlovely Corsican violated neutral territory, lived off the country and made war pay for war by plunder and tribute.

In Napoleon nevertheless were combined all the qualities of patience, daring, coolheadedness and adaptability that combine to make the conqueror. He was an exacting planner, always striving to leave nothing to chance. Yet, when the unforeseen did arise to menace him, he was quick to adjust to it. "What is luck?" he asked scornfully, and replied: "The

ability to exploit accidents." To Thomas Carlyle, Napoleon
was one of the great natural heroes of the race. "There was an
eye to see in this man," Carlyle wrote, "and a soul to dare and
do. He rose naturally to be King. All men saw that he was
such." True, but the hero-worshiping Carlyle might have added
a few more practical reasons for Napoleon's astonishing
success.

The first was that, after he became the autocrat of France
in January, 1800, Napoleon was able to plan his campaigns
in complete command of both the military and political conduct of a war. He was his own cabinet and his own chief of
staff. Once he had staked out his political objectives, he could
take the field to obtain them. The generals opposing him,
always answerable to the chanceries back home, to what old
Blücher castigated as the "despotism of diplomats," had no
such freedom of action. Secondly, Napoleon always fought a
coalition; and coalition warfare, because of the differences in
language, weapons, military customs and even objectives which
customarily divide allies, is the most difficult of all to wage.
In the end, however, Napoleon's very great virtue of holding
within his own mind all the various threads and complexities
of a complicated campaign proved to be his undoing. His
marshals, never quite clear about what he wanted, often
botched his plans. If he had developed a capable staff system
like the Prussian one that humbled France in 1870, he might
not have taken the road to Waterloo.

In the final analysis, however, Napoleonic warfare depended
upon superiority of numbers. In all his great victories, with
the single exception of Dresden in 1813, Napoleon managed
to assemble numbers either superior or at least only slightly
inferior to his enemy. But whenever he could not do so, he
was beaten. It was the mass man and the mass army that
made Napoleonic warfare possible. Napoleon's very speed, the
fury of his assaults, the ruthlessness with which he pressed the
pursuit of a broken enemy, all these depended upon a prodigal

expenditure of human blood and energy. Again and again he combed the classes of older men or called up a year ahead of time entire classes of beardless boys. Napoleonic warfare fed on flesh and blood, and when he was at last defeated and forsaken in 1814 and was crossing southern France into exile, mobs surrounded his carriage to hiss: "Monster! Give us back our children!"

Infantryman and Grenadier, Napoleonic Wars

Nevertheless, all Europe was to make Napoleonic warfare its own. Chief among the evangelizers of this bloody gospel was Antoine Henri Jomini, a Swiss bank clerk who became a Napoleonic general. Jomini also became a Russian general, having nimbly changed sides before the downfall of Bonaparte, and he thus had the advantage of being able to discuss Napoleonic tactics from both sides of the battlefield. Jomini constantly preached the big battle, and his voluminous writings abound in such statements as "Only great general actions can give great results." Clausewitz, a veteran of the Napoleonic Wars from the Prussian side, came afterward, surpassing Jomini not only in his philosophical grasp of the politico-military character of war, but also in bloodthirstiness. "He who uses forces unsparingly, without reference to the bloodshed involved, must obtain a superiority," he wrote. The obvious fact that he who seeks a big battle must be prepared to pay a big butcher's bill was completely acceptable to him. Perfectly logical (one might say cold-bloodedly so), he could go on to say: ". . . there may be cases (for instance, when we have a great superiority in numbers) when the mere diminution of the enemy's forces is an advantage, even if we pay for it by greater loss on our own side."

Here is a perfect defense of Grant in his Wilderness Campaign. He had the superiority of numbers, and though his losses were greater than Lee's, he could better afford them. It is perhaps significant that as Grant fed more and more men into the bloody battles that were actually whittling Lee more than him, he was frequently to be seen whittling grimly on a stick.

Many of our Civil War generals, incidentally, had studied Jomini (though probably not Clausewitz) and shared the European fascination for the Napoleonic creed of the attack and the relentless offensive. They were not aware, as were no generals anywhere, that the development of rifled artillery and the invention of the rifle bullet had conferred a great superiority on the *defense*. This in great part explains the enormous losses of the Civil War. The frightful Confederate carnage at Malvern Hill or the Federal blood bath at Cold Harbor—to name only two such battles—were the consequences of rifled guns. Rifling made firearms more accurate and increased their range. Therefore, an attacker had to advance in full view over a much wider expanse of ground before closing with his unseen, entrenched enemy.

Infantryman, 1870

Unfortunately, this lesson was not only lost on the American commanders of both sides, it was also missed by the Europeans. Helmuth von Moltke, author of the German victory over France in the War of 1870, actually sneered at our Civil War as nothing more than the cross-country scurrying of two armed rabbles. So the Napoleonic tactics of massed assault by mass armies motivated by patriotic passion continued in favor into and through the First World War; and with the inevitable bloody result. By then, the machine gun —to say nothing of much better artillery—and an improved art of entrenching had bestowed an even greater superiority on the defense. Few commanders saw clearly that the problem was now one of how to advance one's own firepower against the firepower of an entrenched army. It was solved, of course, by the tank—a veritable land battleship (as it was originally called) which could plow through a hail of bullets unharmed —and the airplane, which could fly over the battlefield. The solution, however, was never applied. In the end, the British blockade brought Germany to her knees, and the entry of fresh American troops and industrial power bowled her over.

Therefore, war that had been immobilized and stalemated by rifled guns, was made fluid and mobile again by the tactics of the blitzkrieg and the high American art of amphibious warfare. In Korea, tactics fluctuated between those of position or mobile warfare according to the political objectives of the belligerents. Amphibious warfare was permissible when MacArthur sought to destroy the North Korean Army with his deep envelopment at Inchon because the United Nations sought to expel the Red invaders from South Korea; and because the UN also sought to unify all of Korea by force of arms, MacArthur's mobile columns moving up both sides of the peninsula were also permissible. However, after the Communist Chinese entry into the war and the UN desire to limit its spread resulted in a stalemated position, General James van Fleet's desire to open it up again by swinging an amphibious right hook against the east coast of North Korea was vetoed in Washington.

Thus, the evolution of tactics, the chief variables in war because they are so attuned to terrain, weapons, weather and men. Today, tactics have come full cycle; because today in Vietnam the enemy's ambushes and sudden darting strikes, together with our own search-and-destroy operations, are nothing else but a return to the pounce-and-withdraw tactics of predatory animals and primitive men. This is guerrilla warfare, which is now important enough to deserve a chapter of its own.

5. THE "NEW" WARFARE

Although the tactics of guerrilla warfare are probably as old as predatory beasts and primitive men, the art of what is also called irregular or partisan war seems to be a modern innovation. No doubt, there were always guerrillas operating against the fringes of those armies which fought for pay and plunder in the service of the kings and conquerors of the period of Historic Warfare, but these ragged vultures were probably nothing better than bandits. Their motive was strictly to take what could be stolen or ransomed from the persons of unfortunate stragglers, or even to obtain what cruel pleasure they could from torturing or killing them. Even during the early periods of Modern War, a commander might dispatch light infantry or bands of "irregulars" to operate against his enemy's line of communications or to create havoc in his rear. It remained for nationalism and the era of democratic war, however, for guerrilla warfare to take on its peculiar character of a "people's war" against an oppressor or invader.

The word *guerrilla* itself is Spanish. The diminutive of *guerra*, the word for war, it originally meant "little war." Probably it took on its present meaning of organized irregular warfare after the Spanish people used it so effectively to help defeat the French armies of Napoleon in the Peninsula Wars of 1808–14. Proud, fierce and still fanatically devoted to their nation and their Catholic faith, the Spanish were enraged by the presence among them of French soldiers who did not hesitate to desecrate or plunder religious objects. With British support, these Spaniards launched a ferocious "little war" against the French, swooping down on isolated or straggling French detachments and killing and torturing their prisoners. So effective was this guerrilla warfare that the French were compelled to keep large forces in their rear to guard their lines of communication. By the beginning of 1809, nearly three-fifths of the 200,000 French combat troops in Spain had to be employed in such operations, and it was with this considerable assistance that the outnumbered Duke of Wellington eventually was able to defeat the French. What a fitting irony, that the French who had invented popular war were the first to be struck down by a people's war!

They were also the second to be so scourged, during Napoleon's disastrous invasion of Russia in 1812. The dreadful ordeal of the *Grande Armée* at the hands of the Russian people, and in the grip of a cold white vise of a Russian winter, is now so well known that it need not be detailed here; except to say that not 30,000 of the 430,000 men whom Napoleon led across the Niemen River got back to France with him.

Guerrilla warfare may involve mounted irregulars such as the horse commandos* who baffled the British during the Anglo-Boer War of 1899–1902. These mounted riflemen, some 90,000 of them, maneuvered so well over a huge area of 430,000 square miles that the British ultimately were compelled to bring an army of 450,000 soldiers, many of them cavalrymen, into the field against them. Even then the Boer commandos were not subdued until an ingenious network of blockhouses was constructed to fragment the theater of war and thus reduce the mobility of mounted guerrillas. Incidentally, Winston Churchill, who was captured in that war, marked well the effectiveness of the Boer commandos, and it was from this experience that the British Commandos of World War II were born. Here we have an instance of guerrilla warfare being adopted as an auxiliary arm of a conventional army. Our own Army Rangers, as well as the Raider battalions of

---

* "Commando" is the diminutive of the word "command," that is, the force led into the field by its commander.

the Marines, were commandos of this type: small bodies of elite troops organized and trained for sudden raids or daring missions.

And lest we forget, there were also guerrilla horsemen operating during the American Revolution. This war is in some ways a hybrid, a historic watershed standing half in the night of limited kingly war and half in the dawn of unlimited, democratic war. Thus, even before the Spanish innovated guerrilla war, we had outstanding irregular leaders in the persons of Sumter, Pickens and the legendary Francis Marion. These men—and especially Marion, the "Swamp Fox"—were able to keep Patriot resistance in the South alive until Washington could spare regular forces for that theater. So savagely did the Swamp Fox harry the British with his sudden, lightning raids that they sent an officer to tax him for not meeting them in the open "like a gentleman and Christian." His tactics and his name have been immortalized by William Cullen Bryant in his poem "Song of Marion's Men":

> Woe to the English soldiery
> That little dread us near!
> On them shall light at midnight
> A strange and sudden fear:
> When, waking to their tents on fire,
> They grasp their arms in vain,
> And they who stand to face us
> Are beat to earth again;
> And they who fly in terror deem
> A mighty host behind,
> And hear the tramp of thousands
> Upon the hollow wind.

From another poet, the Chinese Communist chieftain Mao Tse-tung, comes another metered guerrilla credo, expressed in sixteen words:

> Enemy advancing, we retreat;
> Enemy entrenched, we harass;
> Enemy exhausted, we attack;
> Enemy retreating, we pursue.

Falling back on prose, which actually is sturdier and more serviceable for fighting, like a Roman short sword, Mao writes: "In guerrilla warfare, select the tactic of seeming to come from the east and attacking from the west; avoid the solid, attack the hollow; attack, withdraw; deliver a lightning blow, seek a lightning decision. . . . In guerrilla strategy, the enemy's rear, flanks and other vulnerable spots are his vital points, and there he must be harassed, attacked, dispersed, exhausted and annihilated."

Obviously, the one thing an irregular leader seeks to avoid is a massed, front-to-front battle with a modern army. So he turns the resources of favorable terrain and sympathetic population against this powerful foe. Because guerrilla warfare is usually fought on foot, the importance of terrain cannot be too strongly stated, for partisan warfare probably would not be possible in a desert or a prairie, areas in which there is little chance for cover and concealment. Generally, unsettled and irregular terrain is most amenable, and particularly heavily forested mountains. Guerrilla warfare probably is possible in cities, judging from the success of the so-called Stern Gang in their activities against the British in Palestine shortly after World War II. Citified guerrilla warfare, however, even more than the type waged in the country, must depend upon the second condition of a sympathetic population. The guerrilla must be able to melt back into this population merely by dropping his gun and putting on either a mechanic's overalls or a peasant's smock.

A minority, however, cannot melt back into a majority. An invading army, of course, is a minority, clearly marked out by its language and customs, if not by its uniforms. So is a racial minority. Proponents of Black Power among us who advocate such a course simply do not understand that a man's coloring is a kind of biological uniform that he cannot put off. If a minority identifiable by its race or color begins a guerrilla war against the similarly identifiable majority, it invites suicide. This biological uniform of race has certainly been an additional difficulty for the Americans fighting their war of counter-insurgency in Vietnam.

It is also, incidentally, the more practical explanation for the failure of Americans to escape their Communist captors in the Korean War. With their big noses and black or white skin they had absolutely no chance of moving undetected through a country populated by people with small noses and tan skin. If an army of Asians were to invade America, how would it be possible for their captive soldiers to move, say, from a Great Lakes prison camp to their own army's positions on, say, the Pacific Coast? For the same reason, we, not they, would have the opportunities for waging guerrilla warfare. Concealment, then, is the absolutely basic condition of guerrilla warfare; it is as necessary as air to men or water to fish.

Obviously, concealment depends upon the allegiance of the people inhabiting the theater of war. In national guerrilla wars such as the Spanish and Russian, this was almost taken for granted. No one needed to teach the Spaniards or Russians to hate the French invader. This was not exactly so of the Vietminh's guerrilla warfare against the French colonialists in 1946–54, because some parts of the population remained loyal to the French and many Vietnamese served in the French forces. It is even less true of the "national war of liberation" being fought at present in South Vietnam. There, both the North Vietnamese–Viet Cong and the American–South Vietnamese coalitions are striving to gain the allegiance of the people; the Communists hoping either to compel it by a campaign of calculated terror or to induce it by military success and propaganda, the Americans and their allies by denying the Communists military success and by a program of "nation building."

At this writing (August, 1969) neither side seems to have been successful, and the mere fact that the Communists may still rely upon the support of the population of the areas which they control seems to illustrate a second, vital fact in guerrilla warfare. This is that you cannot sever a guerrilla lifeline. A deep envelopment such as MacArthur's at Inchon would have been of much less value if the North Koreans had possessed the sympathy of the South Korean population. MacArthur would have isolated them from their own base well enough, but he might also have "stranded" them in a sea of sympathy. Therefore, any landing above the 17th parallel followed by a drive to the Laotian border might very well cut the enemy's supply and reinforcement lines, but it would not have the same effect as MacArthur's master stroke in Korea.

To repeat the image that the guerrilla is the fish and the people the water in which he swims, if that "water" is warm and friendly, it will provide the guerrilla with food, intelligence, concealment and recruits; if it is cold and hostile, it will leave him starving, naked and exposed. Ultimately, then, the aim of guerrilla warfare is to drown the enemy in a sea of hostility.

Thus, it is the means by which the weak may weary and whittle the strong. It is simplicity versus sophistication, as in the pongee sticks of the Viet Cong versus our own helicopter gun ships; or guile versus gadgetry, as when guerrillas in peasant dress safely infiltrate outposts guarded by radar, or when camouflage thwarts aerial photography. With such methods, the Communists hope to gain the allegiance of the countryside and isolate the cities. Actually, this is the very tactic with which Asian Communism seeks to gain world dominion. Lin Piao, Mao Tse-tung's chief lieutenant, has repeatedly compared the nations of Western Europe and North America to the "cities" and the backward populations of Asia, Africa and Latin America to the "countryside." Seize this "countryside" and inflame it against the "cities," he declares, and the world will be won for Communism.

Actually, Lin's theory is not new. It is only a reformulation of basic Marxist doctrine on the class war. By "countryside"

Lin really means "rural population." He means the "people" who are to be enlisted in the class war against the "ruling classes." When this point is accepted, the enemy Tet Offensive of 1968, as well as the renewed attacks on cities in early 1969, becomes clear. The Communists probably attacked the cities because of the enormous population shift which took place in South Vietnam after the American armed intervention in 1965. Finding that the people were fleeing the country for the cities, the Communists may have been compelled to launch what was in reality a counterattack against an unforeseen social upheaval. So it is the people's allegiance (or at least their support, voluntary or involuntary) which is the true objective of revolutionary guerrilla warfare.

To obtain it, the Communists talk as hard as they fight, for one of the chief characteristics of revolutionary guerrilla warfare is its strong emphasis on propaganda—a subject to which this study will now turn.

6. THE LIE, THE WHOLE LIE, AND NOTHING BUT THE LIE

War propaganda has three purposes: to unify one's own people, to subvert the enemy's and to enlist the support of neutrals. War propaganda, of course, plays on the passions of a people. It is intended to inflame one's own with hatred of the enemy, to infect the enemy's people with pessimism or distrust of their leaders and to create sympathy among the uncommitted peoples. Generally, it is less effective in professional or mercenary war than in ideological or popular war. Men fighting for pay or plunder usually cannot care less whether their enemy is or is not the devil incarnate. But in a religious war, such as the jehads of Islam or the Crusades of Christendom, the troops generally are driven by a religious zeal often excited by the arts of propaganda. The brutal soldiery of the Thirty Years' War who drove the peasants of the rival faith into burning barns were also motivated by propaganda, and so powerful was their religious hatred that they considered the incineration of innocent bystanders less reprehensible than to spike out the eyes of a statue of the Virgin or to profane a Lutheran chapel.

Frederick the Great knew well the value of propaganda. "If we are in a Protestant country," writes this cynical atheist, "we wear the mask of protector of the Lutheran religion, and endeavor to make fanatics of the lower order of people, whose simplicity is not proof against our artifice. In a Catholic country, we preach up toleration and moderation, constantly abusing the priests as the cause of all the animosity that exists between the different sectaries, although, in spite of their disputes, they all agree upon material points of faith."

Frederick's cynicism, however, sounds positively puckish or even starry-eyed alongside the snarling, foaming hatreds cooked up by the calculated propaganda of the revolutionary French. For the fathers of popular war were also the founders of the war propaganda techniques still in use today. Much as we may like to accuse the Communists or the Fascists of originating the devices of "indoctrination" or "brainwashing," the fact is that one and three-quarter centuries ago the same methods were being used to carry out Carnot's command to "preach hatred of kings."

Before every major operation, the conscripted troops of the Revolutionary armies were assembled to be worked upon by inflammatory orators, while other agents circulated among them to encourage the fiery or intimidate the lukewarm. Next, women served out brandy, and as the battlefield began to echo to cheers for the Republic and curses for kings, military bands began to play martial music. After this, according to the Royalist officer Mallet du Pan, ". . . fifty thousand savage beasts, foaming at the mouth with rage and yelling like cannibals, hurl themselves at top speed upon soldiers whose courage has been excited by no such passion." Eventually, of course, the French soldiery became so inured to and disgusted by the fomentations of the harpie agents of the Convention that one unit actually despatched a group of prisoners to the interior with the sarcastic comment that the Convention might eat them if they liked.

In fact, the revulsion against the Revolution's propaganda techniques was general. Even Napoleon refrained from inciting the Russian peasants against the Czar, and the Duke of Wellington had a positive horror of fomenting rebellion in a foreign country. In 1871, Bismarck coldly turned his back upon the revolutionaries of the Paris commune. But then, in 1914, when Europe went mad with militarism and democratic war returned with a vengeance, propaganda became a prime military weapon. Of all its practitioners, the British were the most adept; and it is not too much to say that British propaganda was at least as effective as the British blockade or the French Army in bringing about the downfall of Germany. First, British propaganda (coupled with the German undersea war, of course) drew America into the war. Then, British propaganda began to undermine German morale while American propaganda (Wilson's famous Fourteen Points were originally advanced as a clever propaganda pitch) succeeded in separating the German leadership from the people. And as much as we might be nauseated by the Hate Sessions of Orwell's *1984,* the fact is that in America in 1917–18 there were no less than 75,000 "Four-Minute Men" trained to spew out four minutes of undiluted hatred of the Germans at movie houses and public halls across the country. The British, who once thought of the Germans as cousins, were also so skillfully trained to "hate the Hun" that even Winston Churchill has confessed that he could not possibly have stood for re-election on any other platform but "the gallows for the Kaiser."

War propaganda became an even more perfect art in the hands of the dictators, and Hitler's conquests in the Low Countries, France and Scandinavia were in great part made possible, as all the world now knows, by the seeds of subversion sown by his "fifth columnists." That phrase, incidentally, was coined during the Spanish Civil War when one of Franco's generals advancing on Madrid was asked if he expected to take the city with only four columns. "No," he replied. "I have a fifth column within the city." Hitlerite propaganda, of course, provided Germany with internal stability by furnishing the Jewish scapegoat, and also, through the myth of the "pure, Aryan race," by investing every last German with a patent of nobility. "Pure of blood every Ass wants to be now," Cervantes wrote mockingly of the numerous hidalgos of his own romantic Spain, and Hitler played skill-fully on the same vanity. The Bible, as Rousseau tartly observed, may be barren of any reference to "King" Adam or "Emperor" Noah, but the fact is that the Common Man's unquenchable thirst for noble lineages and family crests has been the making of many a clever charlatan. Benito Mussolini also used this sort of flattering propaganda to give weary Italy a rich transfusion of blue blood. No one passed out more medals and decorations than the Duce, and in 1937 he carried this artful absurdity to its sublime peak when he declared that the prize for the most outstanding journalistic performance of the year should go to three Italian reporters who had whistled derisively at the Emperor Haile Selassie as he attempted to plead Ethiopia's cause before the League of Nations. According to the citation, this intrepid trio had "defended the honor of Italy and the whole of Western civilization."

Inane as this may seem to us now, it was effective then. So too were the seemingly imbecilic tactics of the Chinese and North Korean Communists when the truce talks began at Kaesong. An intelligent man might laugh at the idea of providing a chair with sawed-off legs for Admiral Joy of the UN truce team, but when the Admiral was photographed gazing upwards into the eyes of General Nam Il (who was actually a foot shorter than Joy) the ruse created the desired effect of the vanquished on his knees before the victor. Generally, the Asian masses are not too knowledgeable; and so, when the Communist truce negotiators coolly decorated the record with the bald lie that Russia rather than the United States had really defeated Japan, they were probably believed at home.

This is the age of Newspeak and Doublethink: "Peace is War. Freedom is Slavery. Ignorance is Knowledge." But it was not Big Brother who first perceived that a population at the mercy of controlled communications is easily deceived. In the Sinai War of 1956, for instance, when Egypt was soundly beaten in the desert by Israel and invaded at the Suez

Canal by the Anglo-French, the fact that these hostile forces were eventually withdrawn upon the insistence of the United States provided Premier Nasser with the opportunity to proclaim a "victory." He was believed, of course, just as Santa Anna was believed after he came home to Mexico City in 1847 to request that a *Te Deum* be sung to celebrate his "victory" over the Americans at Buena Vista.

Deception is not always the monopoly of police states, however. In 1959, President Eisenhower publicly denied that a U-2 high-altitude reconnaissance plane had violated Soviet airspace, sticking firmly to his story until the Soviets produced the rather undeniable person of the downed pilot. Even in a free society such as ours, where dissent and criticism are constitutional guarantees, there is the danger of believing one's own propaganda. Thus, when Fidel Castro in 1961 repeatedly warned his people and the world that Cuba was about to be invaded by "Yankee imperialist lackeys," few people in the States believed him until the day of the Bay of Pigs.

In the Cold War as well as in hot wars, then, it seems true that the truth is always the first casualty; and it is probably a good idea to doubt the reports of even a victorious general. The temptation to clarify an impossible confusion or to discredit Lady Luck is sometimes irresistible. Thus, after the lucky Blücher had won the Battle of the Katzbach, he said to Gneisenau: "The battle we have won, nobody can deny us that; but now I wonder how we shall go about making the people understand how cleverly we have devised it."

Napoleon was probably one of the world's most artful writers of communiqués designed to glorify and exaggerate his own part in an engagement. The heroic-size oil paintings decorating the Hall of Battles in Versailles are tributes to the Corsican's astute sense of what would today be called "dressing up one's image." History has always thrilled to that splendid spectacle of the fiery young Corsican seizing a flag to lead the decisive charge across the bridge at Lodi, when in fact it was Berthier who did it while Napoleon was occupying a ditch. But Napoleon's report on that battle not only exalted Paris, it convinced the author that he was in fact a man of destiny! As he was to say later: "The power of words on men is astonishing." Thus, his eve-of-battle speeches and general orders are often masterpieces in the art of inspiring an army, and it has always been a little heartbreaking to discover that many of them—especially the splendid address to the Army of Italy—were actually dictated years later in the comfort of his second exile on St. Helena. Eve-of-battle speeches, incidentally, are another form of propaganda, one which has not always profited from the sharp psychological insights of a Bonaparte. Wellington despised the form, and claimed that the worst he heard came from an old Portuguese general who assembled his division and growled: "Men, remember one thing—remember that you are Porrrrtuguese!"

Yet, if the victor is to be doubted, how much more the vanquished? The rub here, of course, is to find cause to suspect that the general is, in fact, fibbing. Take Douglas MacArthur's gloss on the only defeat of his remarkable career: the repulse dealt his "win-the-war" offensive by the Communist Chinese in Korea. MacArthur described this full-scale offensive as a "reconnaissance-in-force" designed to "reach up" to the Yalu "and spring the Chinese trap." Here is a masterpiece; and yet, the Japanese generals and admirals of World War II were probably even MacArthur's superiors in compelling defeat to cough up victory at pen point.

Probably because they were the products of a society in which the only acceptable apology for failure is frequently suicide, and where saving face is almost as important as saving the day, the Japanese often minimized their reverses or magnified their successes. Thus, it was not until the end of the war that the Japanese Army learned of the Navy's disastrous defeat at Midway; and even though Premier Tojo was informed of the battle's outcome, he never knew the details.

In the present time, the uses of propaganda are more positive. In February, 1968, when the Viet Cong opened their Tet Offensive, some of their units were equipped with broadcasting tapes announcing that the South Vietnamese Army was fighting with them against the Americans. Obviously, if the Communists had been able to put this false message on the air waves, it would have had a deeply divisive effect upon South Vietnam. In warfare fought to gain the allegiance of the people, the importance of propaganda is obvious. Sometimes the Communists value a propaganda victory as much as or more than a battlefield victory. Battles will be planned with the objective of making a great psychological impact somewhere else. Dienbienphu is the prime outstanding example of this technique. No more than 16,000 French troops were engaged there against perhaps 40,000 Vietminh, and as battles go this was certainly not a "big" one. But it loomed large in the minds of the French people, if only because a carefully nourished propaganda campaign at home made it appear that all depended on holding Dienbienphu. The French Communists and Socialists who had once been the friends and tutors of Ho Chi Minh in his days as a world traveler had already organized a successful antiwar campaign in which war widows were mocked and war-wounded men spat upon, so that a war-sick and divided France needed only one more shock to cause her to throw up her hands in despair. This came at Dienbienphu, and although I am not one of those who would have desired a victory for French colonialism in Vietnam, I still think it necessary, if I am to explain how the Communists use propaganda as a war weapon, to include this undoubted showpiece.

It is possible that the Communists' unsuccessful siege of Khesanh in 1968 was also intended to strike a psychological blow. Certainly, the emphasis which American communications gave to the plight of that outpost invested it with a significance far beyond its true value. The fact that it was held by American Marines, invincible in battle for nearly 200 years, also induced many people on the home front to hold their breath in agony. Nor is it too much to suggest that when Khesanh was finally relieved, you could virtually *hear* the American public sighing aloud in relief. And yet, when the area around Khesanh was explored, it was discovered that the enemy had nothing like the heavy concentration of troops that had been reported.

Nevertheless, American communications, whether Cassandran, capricious or merely uncritical, had created in the American consciousness a dread sense of another Dienbienphu impending. Again and again, Khesanh was compared to the French calamity of that name. And then what? Came the Tet Offensive, the furious Communist onslaught upon the chief cities of South Vietnam, and it may not be too much to suggest that Tet was General Giap's true design and Khesanh only the loud noise intended to distract Allied troops and concern in that direction. Whether or not this is so cannot be demonstrated yet, and it is really not important for the purpose of this study. What really matters is that enemy propagandists found it so easy to build a developing battle, one that actually was never fought, into a positive bogeyman in the mind of the American public. Our military leaders in Vietnam certainly did not lose their nerve, but quite a few of the folks back home were frightened.

Because it is truer of war than of any other conflict that you become what you fight, we, too, employ the uses of untruth in our counter-insurgency propaganda. The very vigor and coordination of the Tet Offensive sufficed to suggest that General Westmoreland's estimates of enemy capacity were rather too low. One also feels compelled to doubt American figures on enemy casualties. If the Communists actually are losing men at the rate of 3,000 weekly, then North Vietnam is suffering proportionate losses of nearly *twice as many* men as Imperial Germany lost in World War I. For the United

States to suffer proportionate losses we would have to lose 37,500 men weekly or 1,930,000 a year. That is men *killed*. To this observer, it does not seem possible that any nation can endure such attrition among its young manhood for very long.

General Westmoreland has said privately that he considers our casualty figures conservative, declaring: "I have instructions out to everybody that they don't estimate anything, they have to count." But the rending, mangling nature of modern war makes it impossible to count bodies, and it is not likely that many troops are wasting time in the grisly game of matching limbs to torsos. Casualties almost *have* to be estimated, and even though the Americans in Vietnam have worked out a rule-of-thumb scale by which so many captured weapons equals so many enemy dead, this also is merely an estimate; and estimates always contain a large helping of wishful thinking, to say nothing of what happens to them after the estimators come to realize that their battle prowess is judged by the number of enemy they "kill." Anyone who has seen enemy bodies hurriedly bulldozed into mass graves, doused with gasoline, burned and buried will almost automatically doubt the accuracy of battlefield estimates. Only when the war is over do the true figures emerge, if then.

Furthermore, it is impossible to calculate even one's own casualties. A man might be wounded twice on the same day, or he might be evacuated from a battle zone as a non-battle casualty suffering from, say, recurrent malaria, and be classified at the receiving hospital, perhaps through his own eagerness to be awarded a Purple Heart, as a victim of bomb concussion or combat fatigue.

Missing-in-action classifications may also be misleading. A "missing" man may have only decided that this was one battle he wanted to "miss," sailing happily away from an island concealed somewhere on the ship that brought him there. And although there were surely no deserters or men going AWOL (absent without leave) in the jungles of the Pacific, a man listed as missing in the Battle of the Bulge might actually have been a deserter living in Paris.

Finally, if casualty lists are to be distrusted per se, so much more so, in this age of propaganda and organized lying, are immediate reports of the "results" of a battle. It has often been very difficult for a general to determine whether he has won or lost. Usually, the standard test is to declare the side which possesses the field after the fighting is over to be the victor. Yet, a tactical victory can also be a strategic defeat, which is what Pyrrhus meant when, congratulated on his conquest of Fabricius, he took thought of the costs and said: "And a few more such victories will destroy me." The Battle of the Coral Sea in the Pacific was a tactical Japanese victory which was also a strategic defeat. The Japanese inflicted more losses on us than we on them but their attempt to invade New Guinea was repulsed and their timetable of South Pacific conquest delayed. These facts are known now, but they were certainly not grasped then. That is why, again in this age of propaganda, it is still not possible to say whether the enemy's Tet Offensive was a clear-cut victory or defeat. If, as we maintain, the enemy had hoped to bring on a general uprising, then they not only failed but also suffered staggering losses in the process; but if, as they maintain, the objective was to disrupt the pacification program and to dazzle the world with their audacity, as they certainly did in the latter case, and if such purposes are worth the expenditure of 50,000 soldiers, then it was an enemy victory. The rub, of course, is to know for certain what the enemy actually intended to achieve and at what cost; and in this era of calculated deceit, such is not immediately possible.

Propaganda has another insidious and perhaps more harmful drawback, and that is that each side tends to believe its own propagandists. As the game of name-calling and soft-soaping rises in intensity, each side takes these manufactured caricatures for actuality and comes to believe nothing but good of itself and nothing but bad of the enemy. A communications breakdown then ensues, and it is one that is made more difficult to overcome for the second reason that the brainwashed populations—especially those in which there is no free press or open criticism—cannot suddenly be asked to believe that Beelzebub is really not a bad guy after all.

Korea offers the most melancholy proof of what happens when two sides misunderstand and mistrust one another. To them, we were always a "pack of imperialist Wall Street dogs"; to us, they were always "the Communist aggressors." Even though I am convinced that the Communists caused the Korean War, I still believe that if we had let them know that we would not permit them to come south of the 38th parallel, it would not have begun; and if they had made it clear that we would not be allowed north of the parallel, it would not have continued. More than the arts of propaganda, then, it would seem that both sides should cultivate the habit of telling the truth. For if it is important to get along with one's allies, how much more imperative has it now become to understand one's enemy.

7. READER, BEWARE!

Although fighting a war is far from being pleasant, writing about it appears to be unbeatable fun. From time immemorial, writers have found the theme of men in combat irresistible, and it seems safe to say that no other topic (including the subject of sex so fascinating to moderns) has had so much written about it.

Unfortunately, this torrent of words is often a niagara of nonsense. The very popularity of war among writers has only helped to multiply the misconceptions surrounding it; and this is probably because not too many writers have actually experienced battle. (I do not say "war," I say "battle," and the difference is crucial.) As a result, these writers are uncritical and take too many things for granted. And when to this legion of the unlearned is added another army of philosophers, journalists, clergymen, peace advocates, war apologists and poets, all denouncing or defending the institution, as their particular uninformed convictions may move them, the consequence is an appalling expansion of that "fog of war" to which this study earlier alluded. As the sociologist Maurice Davie said of these people: "They have one thing in common: they lack the basis of fact. It is so much easier and more alluring to speculate as to the how and why of war than to grub for the facts."

In war more than in peace, getting the facts is not a simple process. For example: my own comrades of the First Marine Division are still arguing about an enemy tank attack the day of our landing on Peleliu in the Pacific. Some of us (myself

85

included) say that there were Japanese snipers in camouflage dress riding the tanks. Others say this is not true. I said it was so because I saw the snipers, yet a Marine tank colonel who went over the battlefield hours later insists that he found none. He saw, of course, only what he saw. But by the time the colonel arrived on the battlefield there probably *weren't* any snipers around: they were either dead or had fled, having jumped down from the tanks or been shot or pulled from them. Doubtless the colonel reported what he observed, but his testimony should not have been relied upon to disqualify the observations of eyewitnesses speaking of a different point in time. Nevertheless, it was the colonel's version of the tank attack that got into most of the histories, and this may be so merely because his being absent from the battlefield at the moment in question was more than compensated for by his rank. Among some historians, the testimony of rear-rank riflemen, however qualified in time and space, simply cannot overrule that of a man with silver eagles on his shoulders. If the same type of reporter were asked to verify the appearance of St. Peter at the Sanhedrin's trial of Jesus, he would probably prefer interviewing Caiphas or some other high priest to questioning the maidservant who did see Peter and spoke to him.

Small and quibbling as this point may seem, it is of major importance only because it illustrates the melancholy fact that most battlefield reporting is of the second-, third- or even fourth-hand variety. This is because of the obvious fact that no reporter or war correspondent—especially no military historian attempting to *reconstruct* the battle months or even years *afterward*—can be at all the right places at the right time. He is not like a sportswriter, neatly ensconced in his press box, equipped and assisted at every turn in his mission to record the scheduled contest taking place before his eyes. No, he is much more like a police reporter asked to cover a riot erupting in several places at once and spreading in intensity or shrinking into quiescence as it becomes either uncontrollable or controlled. To cover a riot, the veteran police reporter will stick close to police headquarters, the nerve-center of the struggle, the place in which reports are received from on-the-scene policemen and from which orders are issued. Thus, during a battle or a campaign, war correspondents generally stay close to headquarters. There, they are able to see "the big picture" in much the same way that the commanding general beholds it.

Unfortunately, the practice of covering a war from head-quarters puts the correspondent at the mercy of the public relations officer there. It is from the PRO that the correspondent most often receives his information, either at press conferences or briefing sessions or the device of the official printed "handout" which the reporter may pick up on his way to the Officers' Club. Naturally enough, the PRO's job includes keeping the public happy and the enemy guessing. Therefore, he rarely divulges information that will put the commander (his boss) in a bad light, will prove discouraging to the home front or will prove helpful or encouraging to the enemy. Too often, then, the version of a battle which the correspondent is asked to file is the official or "canned" one.

True, there are many veteran correspondents whose understanding of warfare and knowledge of history enables them to read between the lines and to come up with a fairly accurate interpretation of what is actually going on. They also can weigh the canned handout against the information they are able to obtain through contacts and friendships at head-quarters. During the Battle of the Bulge in World War II it appears that more than a few correspondents, both at home and at headquarters, were able to make amazingly shrewd guesses about Hitler's intentions. Unfortunately, they exaggerated the extent of the Nazi success to a degree that led General Eisenhower to remark years afterward: "We were terrified—when we got the papers from the States three weeks later."

And here, in the calamity-howling tendencies of the American press, is another intangible obstacle standing between the general reader and the truth. Doom-saying and decrying appear to be the defect of the high American virtue of self-criticism. A healthy fear of overconfidence sometimes becomes twisted into an irrational overestimate of the enemy. At the outset of the Pacific War, Americans were told that the Japanese were the "greatest jungle fighters in the world," when, in fact, these youths from Tokyo and Nagoya and Nagasaki were actually less at home in the rain forests than the so-called citified Yankees. In Korea, the intervention of the Chinese Communists was described in the States in terms which, by comparison, would have qualified Cassandra for membership in the Optimists' Club. *Time* magazine said, "It was defeat—the worst defeat the United States ever suffered," while *Newsweek* called it "America's worst military licking since Pearl Harbor. Perhaps it might become the worst military disaster in American history. Barring a military or diplomatic miracle, the approximately two-thirds of the U.S. Army that had been thrown into Korea might have to be evacuated in a new Dunkerque to save them from being lost in a new Bataan."

To exaggerate the inaccuracy of these exaggerations is simply impossible, if only because, as events showed, the Chinese Communist attack did not end in victory. The enemy did, of course, blunt MacArthur's win-the-war offensive and thus dealt him a defeat; but they also fell far short of their own objective, which was nothing less than the destruction of MacArthur's forces. When those very same forces turned to confront the Communists again, they brought about the stalemate which still endures—but with South Korea still safely outside the Communist camp. At the time, however, anyone who believed what he had read in the newspapers would have been sadly misled. And this, I say again, is due to a free press's perverted instinct for self-flagellation.

In part, it may also be owing to the public's insistence on

either/or situations. Americans talk too much of "victory" and "defeat." They want to see the situation simplified. But there is nothing more chaotic than a battlefield, nothing more difficult than to tell who has won. Sometimes it may take years after the war is *over* to determine the actual victor. Thus, it is only now clear to students of World War II that if there was any "victor" in that conflict, in the sense of which contestant gained the most from the struggle, it was Soviet Russia. In Korea once again, the North Koreans appeared to have won a decisive victory. They had routed the South Koreans and had repeatedly thrown back the American forces which MacArthur fed into the war piecemeal. In fact, however, the North Koreans lost. The unit-by-unit American intervention had been just enough to delay them, to prevent them from clearing the entire peninsula, and thus to deny them final victory and to give MacArthur enough time and space for the counterstroke that did win the so-called "victory." Victory, yes, until the Chinese Communist intervention.

A victory is the achievement of one's objective. If the objective is the destruction of the enemy's will to fight, then a commander may consider himself the victor when his opponent sues for peace, but not until then. But if one commander falls on his enemy's flank and forces him to withdraw to straighten his lines, he has not won a "victory." He may not have gained more than a temporary tactical advantage, especially if his regrouped enemy comes back at him an hour or a day later. Even if the first commander is left occupying the field, he may not have won a real victory, for it is possible that his opponent may be luring him deeper into hostile or treacherous country. Victory and defeat, then, the true results of a battle or a campaign, generally are only perceived in retrospect; even if the proclamation of one or the other does appear as regularly in our communications media as the daily weather report.

Another regular feature which contributes to the "fog of

war" is the daily war map. Here is the perfection of over-simplification. Those neat black arrows thrusting up toward those tidy black blocks facing down are supposed to represent so many formations of troops moving on the offensive and so many gathered on the defensive, while the shaded area represents "enemy" territory and the white sections are "friendly." But these are nothing more than representations, and at best only representations of tendencies. The map that appears in newspapers and on TV screens is an enormous condensation of the to-and-fro movement of huge masses of men and machines over a vast area that may include a wide variation of terrain, mode of surface transportation and type of building. Moreover, military formations are anything but neat, being easily fragmented by battle, by mismanagement and even by terrain itself. Nor is there really any such thing as "friendly" or "enemy" territory. It is one of the chief defects of maps to suggest possession of territory; this side of the line is, say, totally under water and the other side completely dry. Actually, there are always pools and ponds on the dry side and islands on the wet one. A conquering army never sweeps all before it like a swarm of devouring insects. To refer to Peleliu again, that nasty little island was declared "secured" (i.e., cleared of enemy and safe for occupation troops) in November of 1944, but the last scrawny, starving Japanese soldier did not crawl from his cave until six years later. A map, then, is only the barest suggestion of where the conflict is and how it may be going. To take it for anything more is to think one can explain the Bible by saying it's a book about the Jews and Jesus Christ.

So much, then, for the "fog of war"; and now let us turn to the perhaps more attractive but probably more pernicious problem of the "glamour of war." War is anything but glamorous. Military parades are glamorous, so are military balls and guard mounts; but war is not. War is just what Sherman said it was: "all hell." It is a dreadful compound of tedium

and terror. Yet, when war is portrayed in fiction, it comes
out glamorous. From Homer and the Hebrew prophets to
Victor Hugo, Tolstoy and Hemingway, the romanticizers of
war have managed to invest this institution with a charm
which is the direct opposite of its hideous character. Probably,
this has been unavoidable. Conflict always makes wonderful
reading, and battle the best of all. Any clinical discussion of
war such as Quincy Wright's monumental *A Study of War*
will go largely unread.* Even if the writer does manage to
convey the tedium and the terror of war or the debasement of
a regimented life, the reader really cannot know it. Because
he is experiencing it vicariously, and actually only tasting a
slice of it, he might even find it attractive. Certainly he will
be more impressed by the nobility and self-sacrifice of men in
battle, either shutting out the cowardice, selfishness and
misery or dismissing it as unworthy of himself; and this is
especially true of idealist youth. Moreover, the destruction of
the person and property of "the enemy" of which he reads is
likely to satisfy his own aggressions without the slightest
twinge of conscience.

Perhaps more regrettable than the novelist's tendency to
glamorize war is his less excusable inclination to misrepresent
it. In most cases, this is because the writer does not actually
know battle, or at least has no experience of combat as it was
fought in the period in which his scenes are set. No passage
in literature is more breathtaking than Victor Hugo's description of the charge of the French cuirassiers into the writhing,
kicking, screaming tangle of men and horses that was the
sunken road at Waterloo; and yet, if anything may be said of
this evocative masterpiece, it is that no cavalry charge was
ever conducted in quite that manner. As art it is superb, but
as reality or even probability it is misleading, and this may be
because Victor Hugo did not know war. Leo Tolstoy knew it,

* My own copy of this two-volume work was stamped "Discarded" by
a famous university library simply because it was so seldom requested.

and his *Sevastopol Sketches* written during the siege of that city in the Crimean War are wonderful likenesses of the horrid face of war. Yet, in *War and Peace,* the very artistry of his angel-devil approach to the Napoleonic Wars is historically untrue. Stephen Crane offers the same seeming contradiction. Though slightly overrated, Crane's *The Red Badge of Courage* is an artistic jewel and a gripping story. But it is not really "the way it was"; for that, one must turn to Crane's newspaper reports of the Spanish-American War.

Again, however, the contradiction is only an apparent one. The novelist deals with fiction, with art, which is the perfection of reality. He is selective and concentrated, admitting neither the bizarre nor the anomalous; and he is also larger than life. When the same writer turns historian or reporter, he steps back for a longer look, like a cameraman adjusting his lens from a close-up to a long shot. He tries to get it all in, "tell it like it was." When he does this he is more to be trusted (if the reader is looking for "the truth," i.e., things as they are), even though it is possible more may be learned from him about the "larger truth," the human condition, when he is working as a novelist. As a rule, then, war fiction should never be taken as a handbook of warfare. Men of my own generation reared on the blood-and-sand fiction of Ernest Hemingway were filled with amusement or contempt when they compared his myths with reality. Most GIs thought that the hair on Hemingway's chest seemed to grow a trifle too long.

A third group of writers on warfare—the military historians—also help to glamorize war. Of course, their work does include such particulars as the direction taken by the armies, the number of soldiers involved, the strategic or political background of the war, the caliber of the guns, the maneuvers of the opposing commanders and all those other "cut-and-dried" statistics which, sadly enough, frighten most readers away from military history; yet, even the dullest of plodders may inadvertently allow a call of bugles to escape him, and when he does, he quickens the blood of his reader. He makes war seem exciting, which it can be if one subtracts the long periods of boredom and drill separating the brief moments of exhilaration or exaltation; and charming, which it is not.

Generally, however, it is from the military historian that a reader can learn most about war. Writers of this class usually try very hard to establish what actually happened in any given war or campaign. They consult documents such as general orders, battle plans, minutes of staff meetings, operation maps, aerial photographs, the letters of the participants of all ranks, as well as similar material from the enemy side (if it is available), wherever possible interviewing the combatants, high and low, and studying everything which has been published on the subject. Competent military historians understand war and many of them also know battle, and they take great pains to inform themselves on the political, economic or other factors contributing to a war. Some go over the battlefield itself.

Oddly enough, these "peace-loving" United States of America have produced many topflight military historians, beginning with the peerless Francis Parkman (whom we all quarry when we want to learn of the Colonial Wars) and ending with a rather large crowd of contemporaries such as S. L. A. Marshall, Bruce Catton, Hanson Baldwin and the naval historian Samuel Eliot Morison, to name but a few of the foremost in the field. Unhappily, a new breed of "popularizing" military historian seems to have been spawned since World War II. This is the writer who is constantly on the lookout for the "dramatic," by which he really means the sensational or grisly anecdote, the unverifiable (if not outright invented) quotation, the pointless counterpointing of top-level decisions against small-unit or individual actions, neither of which is located in time or space, but by which the author pretends to trace the course of a battle "at every level." Such writers specialize in interviewing front-line combatants or defeated generals and admirals years or even decades after the event, either searching for "color" or for "new evidence" with which to challenge the "accepted" version of the battle. They do not seem to understand that a soldier who ran away might be interested in placing himself in the forefront of battle, or that defeated commanders, often anxious to vindicate themselves in history, are inclined to slough off the blame on some deceased participant, in the way that Hasso von Manteuffel now holds Hitler responsible for the failure of the Second Ardennes. S. L. A. Marshall has well said: ". . . military historians have discovered through exhaustive trial and error that the witness of badly wounded men about their combat [experience] . . . or of returned POWs on the same subject, or of defeated enemy commanders in the absence of their staffs, was invariably distorted and phantasmagoric, if not glory-seeking."

Usually the work of such "historians" may be identified by the photograph on the back showing the author interviewing some general, after which one may read: "John Something spent seven years gathering the material for this book. He has swum oceans, walked across continents, climbed mountains, forded rivers and twice went thirsty in the Gobi Desert. His travels took him to such unlikely places as a nursing home in Spa (presumably where he met the general) and the Monkey-House at the London Zoo. A five-year-old Belgian girl told him what had caused her father, an American soldier, to desert during the battle. In West Germany, Mr. Something visited a brothel where he discovered what caused the enemy commander to forget to order a critical air strike. Mr. Something even flew to Ireland to interview the famous pro-German Irish rebel leader, Colonel Humility O'Tumulty, and to verify a report that his men mutinied when the Germans gave them English muffins for breakfast. To relive the battle himself,

John Something (a U.S.O. entertainer during the war) slept in countless foxholes, some of them still stocked with *live* ammunition, and vermin-infested cellars. He has crept through abandoned gun positions and bombed-out buildings; and on many occasions, so intense has been his thrust to re-enact the harrowing stories told him by combatants, he has been out after dark." So it goes, a name-dropping, continent-counting masquerade intended to conceal the author's ignorance of war and inexperience of battle; and when you see it, dear reader, beware.

Beware also of that most intriguing form of war literature: the military memoir. Some memoirs are most informative, notably those of Ulysses S. Grant and John J. Pershing—both surprisingly well written—but in the main, memoirs are published as much to influence history as to inform it. They are often apologia. If one were to read only a fraction of the enormous spate of memoirs springing out of World War II, one would be compelled to ask: Who won the war? Field-Marshal Montgomery thinks that General Eisenhower could have crushed the Germans in the West much sooner if he had followed his, Montgomery's, plan for a single, concentrated thrust in the north; General Bradley is quite positive that Montgomery's failure to close the Falaise Gap in France allowed many thousands of Germans to escape; and Winston Churchill, together with his No. 1 soldier, Field-Marshal Lord Alanbrooke, are convinced that the Mediterranean, not Normandy, was the decisive area in which to strike the Nazis.

However much forensic memoirs are likely to prejudice the public and frustrate historians, they are at least entertaining, and much to be preferred to a second type of reminiscence: the one that says nothing. Cardinal Pietro Gasparri, the Papal Secretary of State, has given a splendid definition of this type. Asked to publish his own memoirs, he declined with the remark: "What is interesting, I cannot write; what I can write would not be interesting." Dwight Eisenhower's *Crusade in*

Europe falls into this category. Probably because of Ike's great talent for compromise and his dislike of saying anything wounding of another man, his memoirs are exceptionally dull as well as devoid of information or insights not generally known before they were published. It is as though someone had carefully combed the manuscript for anything interesting or diverting which might have inadvertently gotten past the author, and deleted it.

Finally, we come to the fifth class of war writers: the theorists. These are the least known and by far the most influential. They are the thinkers, the profound students of war and warfare, and just because they are openly evangelical, they are the ones of whom the reader need not beware. Probably the most famous of them is the Prussian soldier Karl von Clausewitz, to whom so many references have already been made in this book.

Clausewitz was a Prussian general who served in many campaigns of the Napoleonic Wars, mostly as a staff officer. He never held command, probably because his thoughtful and perceptive nature was no qualification to lead troops in the field. His masterwork, the three-volume *Vom Kriege* ("On War"), was published after his death. Although written in a heavy, pseudophilosophical style, probably because he wrote at a time when philosophy was in high fashion, *On War* is nevertheless crammed with common-sense observations. It is a handbook not only for generals but for statesmen as well. That is because Clausewitz understood as no one before him that war is an instrument of policy.

"War is only a continuation of State policy by other means," he writes. This is his greatest insight and his most quoted remark, and he repeats it ten dozen different ways. "War is nothing but a continuation of political intercourse, with a mixture of other means." "War can never be separated from political intercourse. . . ." If it is, ". . . we have before us a senseless thing without an object." Again: "War belongs to the province of social life. It is a conflict of great interests which is settled by bloodshed, and only in this is it different from others." The greatest error in war is "to take it for something, or to wish to make of it something, which by the nature of its relations it is impossible to be." Finally: "No War . . . should be commenced without first seeking a reply to the question, What is to be attained by and in the same." In essence, this is Clausewitz's teaching: that war is an instrument of policy. If diplomacy is the carrot of policy, war is the stick. And yet, the one should never be separated from the other. To beat an opponent with the stick of war without asking with the voice of diplomacy if he has had enough would be in Clausewitz's judgment a "senseless thing." War has to have an object, and merely to crush or to annihilate an enemy is no object. Thus the great Prussian, of whom I must unhappily report that he is rarely read. Having studied the memoirs of most American political and military leaders since Clausewitz's day, I have yet to find an allusion to him.

Again unhappily, the same cannot be said for the great American naval theorist, Alfred Thayer Mahan. Captain Mahan was the first president of the Naval War College. He was the world's leading exponent of "navalism," the nautical counterpart of militarism, and his works on the subject have since come to be regarded as the "bible" of sea power. Mahan was the Clausewitz of the waves, and because his arguments were couched in clear, precise and flowing language, he has probably been more widely read and thus more influential than the ponderous Prussian.

With great clarity of insight, Mahan grasped what sea power had meant for Britain, and he argued cogently for a "fleet-in-being." This deep-water navy would require colonies for bases or fueling stations as well as a large merchant marine to trade with the colonies and a huge shipbuilding industry to maintain both navy and merchant marine. Mahan coolly accepted the fact that this was naked imperialism, and in fact, he argued also for an imperialist America, taking up the cry that it was Manifest Destiny for the United States to expand her territories across the oceans. No one was more influenced by these theories than Theodore Roosevelt, who strove mightily to implement them as an assistant Secretary of the Navy (when he helped to start the Spanish-American War) and afterward as President. It was under the impetus of Mahan's arguments, in fact, that America did enter that conflict and embark upon the imperialist career that resulted in the "annexation" of the Philippine Islands.

Another disciple of Mahan's was Kaiser Wilhelm II of Germany, who became so deeply influenced that he challenged Britain for world naval supremacy, a provocation which helped to bring on World War I. From that struggle came a third theorist whose teachings have had a profound effect on warfare. This is the Italian exponent of air power, General Giulio Douhet.

Taking up some of the ideas of the American air officer General Billy Mitchell, Douhet conceived the theory of "strategic bombing." Air power alone could win a war, he argued, by bombing both the enemy's war plant and his population. In fact, Douhet considered the bombing of cities more important than the destruction of factories or armies. It would create chaos and halt production, he said, declaring: "The time would soon come when, to put an end to horror and suffering, the people themselves, driven by the instinct of self-preservation, would rise up and demand an end to the war—this before their army and navy had time to mobilize at all."

Douhet's theories had a powerful effect in Britain, where the first independent flying service, the Royal Air Force, was formed. They also influenced Hermann Goering in Germany and caused the American Army to take its airplanes away from the Signal Corps and create an Army Air Corps. During World War II, both the American and British air chiefs were devout disciples of the theory of strategic bombing, and only reluctantly, toward the end of that struggle, did they accept the incontrovertible truth that the strategic bombing of Germany had *not* broken the German will to fight and had not even reduced German aircraft production. Countries subjected to strategic bombing simply go underground and disperse their people and their war plant, a fact which was given its second and third demonstrations in Korea and Vietnam.

Nevertheless, Douhet's ideas have remained popular, probably because of the irresistible allure of any program promising destruction of the enemy at long range and at no cost to oneself. In the United States, where so many people still believe in the myth that the atomic bomb defeated Japan, one may still find a senator or a general who will advance strategic bombing as the solution to a difficult military situation.

Equally popular, but with good reason, are the theories of two other World War I veterans: Captain B. H. Liddell Hart and Major General J. F. C. Fuller of Britain. These two, incidentally, are representative of the type of military theorist whose writings have a direct effect on battlefield doctrine or tactics. It was from Liddell Hart and Fuller that Hitler's generals learned the tactics of the blitzkrieg, or lightning war.

Liddell Hart developed the style of attack which he called "the expanding torrent." The idea was for commanders to exploit any immediate opportunity, rather than to lose time and surprise waiting for reports to come back from the battlefield. It was based on the principle that "success is usually uneven and progress unequal [and] designed to turn opportunism into a system." Its chief characteristic, of course, was its fluidity.

Major General Fuller's innovation was to recognize that tanks had ended the battlefield stalemate imposed by the superiority conferred on the defense by increased firepower. He believed that tanks and armored troop carriers could win a war by lightning strikes against the enemy's headquarters. The idea was to attack "the brains" of an army, rather than "the body," i.e., the great masses of troops at the front.

With some moderations and adjustments of their own,

Hitler's generals took the ideas of Liddell Hart and Fuller, as well as the theories of other advocates of tank warfare such as Charles de Gaulle of France, and devised their blitzkrieg. When that happened, warfare was opened up again. And then another theorist named Mao Tse-tung came along to close it in once more, or at least to impose the different variety of stalemate already described as revolutionary guerrilla warfare. These are the tactics being employed in Vietnam, and it seems safe to say that out of that conflict a new military theorist will also arise, advancing those seminal ideas which will demonstrate that the pen is still sharper than the sword.

8. HOW TO TELL THE OUTFITS WITHOUT A PROGRAM

In his memoirs, Winston Churchill tells of having suggested to Stalin that perhaps the Pope should be invited to one of their wartime conferences, only to have the cynical Russian Premier reply: "How many divisions does the Pope have?"* Relating this anecdote myself at dinner one night, I was surprised to see the educated wife of an erudite professor respond with a mechanical smile, and then, in a sudden outburst of pique, exclaim: "For God's sake, what *is* a division?"

It is a good question, to which might be added: What is a battalion or a brigade, a squadron or a wing, a flotilla or a fleet? What, in fact, are all these unit designations which appear and reappear in our press during this era of seemingly endless war, and which, to so many Americans, are nearly as incomprehensible as the medieval hunter's quaint catalogues of a pride of lions, a covey of quail or a gaggle of geese?

Obviously, they are the parts of the whole. They are the various subordinate parts into which an army, a navy or an air force must be subdivided in order to solve the problem of command. It should be self-evident that no single commander can exercise direct control over any sizable force. General Eisenhower certainly could not have taken every soldier and sailor in his massive D-Day host and placed each in a particular spot and told each what to do. Having made his general plans and preparations, he issued his general orders to the commanders of his "army groups," who then issued their orders

* When Pius XII heard the story from Churchill, he said, "Tell my son Joseph he will find my divisions in Heaven."

101

to the commanders of their "armies," who issued theirs to their "corps" who finally gave orders to their "division" commanders. Actually, the chain of command goes even much deeper than this, ultimately ending with the sergeant who leads a twelve-man squad; but because each relay of a Supreme Commander's orders to a lower level seems to diminish or distort the original, in the same way that a rumor changes character as it moves from mouth to mouth, formal or written orders usually go no lower than a division.

This is probably because the division is the smallest unit in modern warfare combining all arms—that is, infantry, artillery, armor and engineers, together with service and supply units such as transport and quartermaster, medicine and intelligence. Usually, a division is organized in this way:

DESIGNATION	SIZE	COMMANDED BY
Squad	12 or 14 men	sergeant
Platoon	40 or more men	second lieutenant*
Company	150 or more men	captain
Battalion	800 or 1,000 men	lieutenant colonel
Regiment	3,000 or more men	colonel
Division	15,500 men	major general

The key fighting force of a division is the battalion, usually a force of from 800 to 1,000 men. A battalion is generally composed of three companies, plus a headquarters company; and three battalions form an infantry regiment, while three infantry regiments, together with a regiment of artillery and attached engineers, tanks, service and supply troops and other specialists, combine to make the normal 15,500-man infantry division of the United States Army. Airborne divisions, chiefly because they carry so little armor, are generally smaller and may be less than 14,000 men. Conversely, a mechanized or

---

* First lieutenants, who are one grade senior to second lieutenants, may also command platoons, but more usually serve as executive officers to company commanders, or even as company commanders themselves.

armored division, requiring more tanks, trucks and troop carriers, is larger and may number 16,000 men. Largest of all is the Marine amphibious division, which, with its amphibious tractors, trucks and tanks, as well as its port battalions, is often 20,000 men. Sometimes an amphibious division operating on independent assignment may need to equip itself as a small army. Thus, when the 1st Marine Division landed at Peleliu in September, 1944, it carried its troop replacements with it and numbered a whopping 27,000 men.

During World War I, the American divisions were also very large, being formed of brigades rather than regiments. Each brigade numbered two regiments, and thus, two infantry brigades supported by a brigade of artillery was a six-regiment division of 28,000 men. This huge formation, twice the size of the British, French and German divisions, proved to be most unwieldy in battle; and after the Armistice it was streamlined to roughly its present proportions.

A brigade, incidentally, is a highly flexible unit. Originally, it was a force of 4,000 to 5,000 men and was considered the largest formation over which its commander—a brigadier general—might exercise direct control by the range of his voice. It has had its uses, particularly during the Civil War when the Americans of both sides went along with brigades and regiments* rather than the divisional system introduced by the French Revolution and adopted by most of Europe. Even when Civil War divisions actually were formed by combining regiments or brigades, they had no formal designation such as "9th Infantry" or any permanent organization, but were known by their commanding general's name. The first true division in American history was the 1st Infantry Division formed by Pershing in 1917 and sent to France as the vanguard of the American Expeditionary Force.

* Regular infantry regiments in the Civil War were mostly the three-battalion formations now in use and copied from the French. But the far more numerous volunteer regiments were actually the old ten-company battalions numbering 1,000 men.

The brigade is still useful, especially in an emergency when an available infantry regiment can be made into a miniature army by adding another battalion, as well as supporting artillery, tanks, engineers and aircraft. This was what happened during the dark days in Korea, when the Fifth Marine Regiment on the West Coast was overnight expanded into the 1st Provisional Marine Brigade in this fashion and sent steaming for Pusan. Similarly, the four-battalion 173rd Airborne Brigade was flown to Vietnam in the early days of 1965. When a regiment or battalion is thus beefed up for an independent operation it may be known as a regimental or battalion "combat team." There is also the device of the "task force," by which any special or hastily assembled group may be known by its commander's name. In July of 1950, when it appeared that the North Koreans would drive the South Korean Army into the sea, the 406 soldiers who flew from Itazuke Airfield in Japan to Pusan in Korea as the first American ground troops to enter the war were known as "Task Force Smith" after their commander, Lt. Col. Charles ("Brad") Smith.

Despite all these variations in fighting formations, the battalion remains the basic fighting unit. It is the battalion which ultimately closes with and destroys the enemy, or repulses his assault. Capable of fighting within the framework of regiment or division, the battalion may also operate independently and be supported in the field by aircraft or warships. A division commander entering battle thinks chiefly of how many battalions he has to deploy, and Napoleon, when he wished to make a cynical point, remarked: "God is on the side of the big battalions."

It is also worth noting that among the technocratic, gadget-minded Americans, the proportion of combat battalions to noncombatant is amazingly small. What is called the "division slice," that is, the actual number of soldiers required to keep a division in the field, is roughly 51,000 men. Out of this the actual front-line or "foxhole" strength of a division is no more than 6,000 or 7,000. Thus, the ratio of actual fighting men to service and supply troops is something like 1 to 7 and in Vietnam the actual number of fighting men in March of 1968 was about 80,000 out of the total of 520,000 deployed there. In truth, even when a "combat" division has committed its "combat" battalions, there are few men actually under fire at any one time. This is because of the customary "two up, one back" deployment by which commanders fight their battalions: of his three companies he commits two and keeps one in reserve. In fact, the remark "Two up, one back, hot chow for the troops—and don't trust the other so-and-so on the flanks" seems to be the basic battle lore of most successful commanders.

Thus, when a division is attacking it probably will have only six of its nine infantry battalions in line, and of these battalions only twelve of eighteen companies will be out front, and of these companies only twenty-four of thirty-six platoons, and of these, to carry the example to an extreme that is not always absurd, there may be only forty-eight of seventy-two squads in assault or an actual total of less than 600 of the division's 15,500 men. Reduce this to the number of men in the actual "point" of an assault and it is possible that no more than a few hundred may be under fire. The "grunts" of Vietnam no less than the "GIs" and "Gyrenes" of World War II can still get a sardonic chuckle out of the story about the rifleman who, having been his battalion's actual attacking force throughout a single operation, turned with magnificent disdain upon comrades only a few feet behind him to sneer: "Where were *you* when the stuff hit the fan?"

It is therefore well, when reading battle reports, to understand that a few hundred casualties suffered by this or that American division is probably a greater inroad on its true fighting strength than it would appear to be.

It is also well to be wary of assuming that the "divisions" of other nations are the same size as our own. Generally, they are smaller. Even the divisions of the North Atlantic Treaty Organization may be as low as 13,000 for infantry and 12,700 for armor. Among the Communist Chinese and North Koreans the paper strength of a division was some 10,000, but in actual practice it ranged from 7,000 to 8,500 or less. The Communists also frequently designate some lesser units as a "division" in order to deceive their enemy. Just before the Communist Chinese intervened in Korea, they masked their secret build-up of forces by designating divisions as "battalions," and it appears likely that this ruse was decisive in influencing American intelligence's incredibly low estimate of the enemy's strength. In Vietnam, enemy divisions have been roughly the same size as those of the Communist Chinese, who were, after all, the military mentors of the Vietminh.

Difficult as it is to establish division strength accurately, it is still harder to be certain of the higher formations of corps, army, army group and finally expeditionary force. Generally, two or more divisions form a corps which, with its own special troops such as heavy artillery and headquarters, usually numbers 40,000 or more men and is commanded by a major general. Two or more corps form an army of about 100,000 men or more, usually commanded by a lieutenant general, and two or more armies make an army group customarily commanded by a full general. An expeditionary force such as the one commanded by Pershing in World War I or the one commanded by Eisenhower in the second global conflict can be numbered in the millions and rates a five-star General of the Army, the American equivalent of a marshal, as its commander.

Even above the expeditionary force is what is now called a "theater of war." Originally, the theater of war was considered that area in which one could strike at the enemy.

Usually, it included entire countries, coastlines and the ocean itself, as well as those neutral nations whose alliance or sympathy was to be elicited through terror, diplomacy or propaganda. With the advent of total war and air power, however, it was necessary to divide the whole warring world into theaters. Thus, while the Germans and the Russians were engaged on the Eastern Front during World War II, the Western Allies alone set up five distinct theaters or "areas." They were the European under Eisenhower, the Mediterranean under, first, Eisenhower and then Field Marshal Sir Henry Maitland Wilson, the China-Burma-India under Admiral Lord Louis Mountbatten, the Southwest Pacific under MacArthur and the Pacific Ocean under Fleet Admiral Chester Nimitz, who also commanded the Pacific Fleet. (MacArthur, incidentally, did *not* lead the Americans to victory over Japan, as some responsible publications still seem to suppose. He was one of two area commanders, and his contribution toward the Japanese defeat was actually smaller than Nimitz's. Throughout the early years of the war MacArthur agitated for a single Pacific commander, but as soon as he was informed that if the job were created it would go to Nimitz, he not only dropped his campaign but also considered resigning. It is likely that the myth of MacArthur the Pacific Chief comes from the fact that, because he had been chosen to direct the occupation of Japan, it was he who accepted the Japanese surrender. It is also likely that legend-slaying simply did not interest Nimitz, an unusually modest admiral who consistently, and with humorous disdain, resisted all appeals to publish his memoirs.)

At any rate, a theater commander is supreme within his area, and all the forces there—land, sea and air—are his to command. He is responsible only to his chiefs of staff or general staff, as the case may be. Among allies there may be a still higher echelon such as the Combined Chiefs of Staff which functioned for the Anglo-American coalition in World

War II. In turn, the military chiefs are responsible to the civilian political power.

Up until 1947, the American military establishment had been divided between the War Department (Army and Army Air Force) and the Department of the Navy (Navy and Marine Corps), each headed by a civilian secretary with Cabinet status and directly responsible to the President as commander in chief.* In 1947 the National Security Act reorganized the military, giving the Air Force independent status and setting up apparatus to coordinate national security. On the civilian side it created the National Security Council, the Central Intelligence Agency responsible to that Council and the National Security Resources Board. On the military, it provided for a National Military Establishment headed by a civilian Secretary of Defense appointed by the President. Under the Secretary of Defense were the separate Departments of the Army, Navy and Air Force, each with its own civilian secretary. Next came the Joint Chiefs of Staff, the uniformed chief officers of the Army, Navy and the Air Force. Sometimes, when the chiefs meet to discuss matters affecting the Marines, the Commandant of the Marine Corps is present.

The Marines, although a part of the Department of the Navy, being actually a naval army, are organized almost exactly like the Army. The Navy and Air Force, of course, are entirely different.

Navies are rarely as tidily divided and subdivided as an army, and their organization has varied according to the type of ship which ruled the waves and around which the various "fleets" or "squadrons" were assembled. Today, the "fleet" system is in use. A fleet is a large body of ships of all sizes, and a formally numbered or named fleet, such as the 7th

---

* The Coast Guard is a service of the Department of the Treasury. In time of war, it operates as part of the Navy, or at the direction of the President.

Fleet or Asiatic Fleet, usually is subdivided into "divisions." Thus, its total submarine force would be divided into so many numbered divisions of from four to a dozen vessels apiece.

The word "flotilla" which often appears in military history seldom has the formal fixed meaning of a numbered or named formation. A flotilla is merely a small group of small ships. Thus, if one wished to describe two or more sub-chasers or destroyers, one would use the word "flotilla." One would never, however, so describe a formation of battleships or cruisers. For this the word "squadron" is used. A squadron, incidentally, once had the formal, fixed meaning of today's "fleet." Thus, when Dewey sailed to Manila Bay in 1898 he led the United States Asiatic Squadron, but when Admiral Thomas Hart commanded naval forces in the same waters in 1942, he led the U.S. Asiatic Fleet.

To make matters still more confusing there is a "task force," such as the famous "Task Force 38" with which the jaunty Admiral Halsey promenaded the coast of Japan in 1944, or a "force" such as "South Pacific Force" which wrested Guadalcanal from Japan two years earlier. In 1943, however, the U.S. Navy adopted the "fleet system," providing odd-numbered fleets for the Pacific, even-numbered ones for the Atlantic. These were again divided into task forces, groups and units.

An air force, a relatively recent military organization, is comparatively simple in its organization. In America, the United States Air Force is divided into various named or numbered "commands" or "forces," which are again divided into wings, groups and squadrons. A squadron is the basic formation, being composed usually of no less than six and as many as two dozen aircraft. There are also the noncombat components of a wing, such as the supply group or food service squadron. A squadron may also be subdivided into "flights" of four airplanes or more. This table of organization is also followed in the air arms of the Navy and Marine Corps, although naval air officers have naval rank. In the table that follows, Army, Air Force and Marine officers are ranked by the titles on the left, those in the Navy by those on the right.

RANK	INSIGNIA*	RANK
General of the Army	Five Stars	Admiral of the Fleet
General	Four Stars	Admiral
Lieutenant General	Three Stars	Vice Admiral
Major General	Two Stars	Rear Admiral
Brigadier General	One Star	Commodore (seldom used)
Colonel	Silver Eagle	Captain
Lieutenant Colonel	Silver Leaf	Commander
Major	Gold Leaf	Lieutenant Commander
Captain	Two Silver Bars	Lieutenant
First Lieutenant	One Silver Bar	Lieutenant (Junior Grade)
Second Lieutenant	One Gold Bar	Ensign

* The Marine Corps does not rate a five-star general. Also, these insignia are worn on the shoulders and shirt collars; in the Navy, with its stripe insignia on the sleeves and shoulders, officers are also ranked in this way: ensign, one stripe; lieutenant (j.g.), one and a half stripes; lieutenant, two; lieutenant commander, two and a half; commander, three; and captain, four.

9. THE ARMS RACE: FROM ALCHEMY TO ATOM

In the days of Primitive and Historic Warfare, weapons were either edged or pointed and basically limited to sword and spear, ax and arrow, however marvelously they might differ in design. In our age, oddly enough, the choice of weapons became even more limited until (if one considers bayonets as merely supplemental and excepts the numerous varieties of hand bomb which we call a grenade) there was no choice at all but only the single and all-encompassing gun. True enough, our own times have witnessed the appearance of aerial bombs delivered to target by gravitational pull, as well as the self-propelled missiles called rockets; nevertheless, in all but the last ten years of Modern Warfare, battles have been fought with this single device of propelling an object or a substance through a tube. In a word, with guns.

Although guns seem to be all but endless in their variations, there are basically only two types: the handgun of the foot soldier, his side arms or shoulder weapons, his "small arms" known as pistols and rifles, and the heavier artillery (from the French *artiller*, to fortify or equip), called "crew-served" weapons because they require more than a single soldier to operate them. Two there are, then, and of all the facets of the study of warfare, there is none more fascinating than the evolution of firearms.

In the beginning, however, the emphasis was upon cannon, and the first of these "crew-served" weapons appears to have been a "handgun." Around 1380 there were cannon weighing as little as 25 pounds which could be held and aimed by a

111

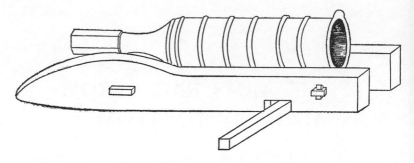

Bombard, Late Fourteenth Century

single man. They were named bombards or culverins (from the Latin *colubra* or "serpent" for the way they spat fire and smoke). Constructed of wood planks bound by iron hoops, they looked like and were called "barrels," the word still in use today to describe a gun tube. In another fifty years, however, these little demons were massive monsters weighing up to three tons and capable of hurling 40-pound balls a distance of 1,400 yards. Seldom cast in a single piece, they were made of wrought-iron bars welded together to form a hollow tube which was bound together by hoops. At first, they fired stones or iron spears, and when the Moslem Turks stormed Constantinople in 1453—the date generally accepted as the dividing line between the Middle Ages and the Modern period—they were equipped with cannon which could throw stones up to 600 pounds. Stones, however, were unreliable missiles which needed to be chipped and shaped to fit the gun barrel, and they were quickly discarded in favor of solid iron balls.

By then, gunsmiths had learned to cast gun barrels with smooth tubes or "bores," and the cannon balls also had to be cast smooth so that they would not jam and burst the barrel. A burst gun, incidentally, was a common occurrence on either training ground or battlefield, and the first distinguished victim of his own fickle "artyllaire" seems to have been James II of Scotland. At the siege of Roxburgh in 1460 he stood near a cannon "that brake in the shuting, by the which he was stricken to the ground and died nastilie."

In the sixteenth century, a carriage was developed by which artillery became mobile. Guns were fitted to a two-wheeled axle attached to a heavy wooden beam or "trail" which projected to the rear. To move them, a second set of wheels known as a "limber" could be rolled under the trail and attached to it and the entire four-wheel carriage harnessed to a team of horses. In the same era King Henry VIII of England passed an ordinance or law specifying gun weights. These cannon,* known as "ordinance guns," came to be called ordnance after the *i* was dropped, and soon all artillery was spoken of by that name. By then also, "Artillerie, th' infernall instrument, New brought from hell to scourge mortalitie, with hideous roaring and astonishment," had begun to sweep all before it. Feudalism (and chivalry as well) lay in a heap of shards that had once been baronial strongholds. The kings, in company with their master gunners, were all-powerful.

Frequently these gunners were civilians who rented out both their cannon and services for a fee. They kept their "secrets" to themselves and looked down upon the foot soldiers, who in turn scorned the gunners as rather ungallant bookworms. In truth, artillery, like the engineers, was one of the intellectual arms of warfare, and mathematicians were already at work calculating the forces which would take a missile straight to its target. During the Thirty Years' War, however, artillerists lost their civilian status and were enrolled in the army as professional soldiers like the infantry, cavalry and engineers.

---

* Although there were still many different forms of artillery, guns had become divided into two general forms: the shorter cannon firing heavy shot a short distance, the longer culverins firing a smaller shot a longer distance. Eventually, however, the word cannon came to mean all big guns, and that is the meaning intended here.

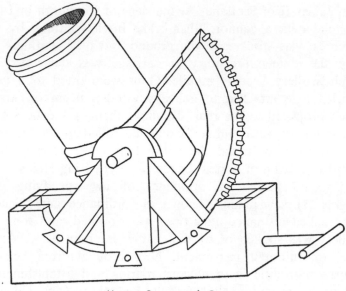

Mortar, Seventeenth Century

During that seventeenth century, under the impact of the wars of Louis XIV of France, two new types of artillery appeared: the mortar and the howitzer. Both are high-angle fire weapons, meaning that their trajectory or path of flight is a looping up-and-down one rather than the flat low flight of conventional cannon. The mortar (named for the apothecary's bowl) is a short-range gun with a trajectory so high that it can fall on an enemy behind a hill, and some modern mortarmen boast that they can drop a shell down a chimney. Resembling nothing so much as a stovepipe, this unlovely killer remains the terror of infantrymen everywhere; and it is safe to say that mortars have maimed and killed more human beings than any other weapon devised—including the atomic bomb. A howitzer's high-angle trajectory is not quite so steep, and it is a longer-range gun. Although it cannot be carried and mounted by hand like a mortar, it is still light enough for use in mountainous terrain. Despite these inventions, however, cannon had not been radically changed. They were still loaded at the "muzzle," or mouth of the gun, by pushing a charge of powder down the tube after which the cannon ball was rammed home and the gun fired by placing a match to a touchhole leading to the powder charge in the base of the gun.

The first real technical improvement came in 1739 when a Swiss cannon-maker named Maritz cast his guns solid and bored the tubes after they had cooled. From this process also the inside of a gun tube came to be known as the "bore." Its effect on the mass production of guns was enormous, and after horse artillery was organized in the last decade of the eighteenth century, that is to say after every soldier in an artillery company—gunner, assistant, ammunition carrier or officer—was mounted on a horse, the scene had been prepared for the advent of the greatest artillerist of all time: Napoleon Bonaparte.

At the age of twenty-three, Napoleon's genius as a gunner put the port of Toulon at the feet of the Republic, and three years later—in 1796—he commanded the entire French Army. Better than any captain before him, and few since, Napoleon knew that cannon kill men. He deliberately expanded and packed his batteries until he had a gun proportion of 4 cannon to every 1,000 men. He also copied the caliber of his enemy's cannon so that he might shoot captured ammunition. Finally, instead of using his guns merely to bombard the enemy before the assault or to cover a withdrawal, he massed his batteries to deliver a converging fire which would actually tear a hole in his enemy's lines. His "case shot," shells filled with bullets which sprayed a given area upon bursting, struck down enemy soldiery like tenpins.

Case shot, introduced in 1410, was the forerunner of what today is called canister. It is simply buckshot on a large scale, a cylindrical can of pellets fired at close range to burst open and spray a wide area. For intermediate distances of 800 to

1,000 yards there was also "grape," a cluster of larger balls clamped together between wooden disks. It was of this which the young Napoleon spoke when he sneered that "a whiff of grape" would scatter the revolutionary mob outside the Tuileries and save the monarchy. The long-range variation of case shot, and the deadliest of all, has entered history under the name of its inventor, General Sir Henry Shrapnel of Britain.

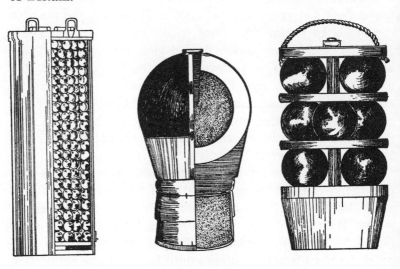

Types of Artillery Ammunition
Left: case shot or canister; center: shell;
right: grapeshot

An improvement in ammunition gave Shrapnel his opportunity. For centuries after the invention of gunpowder, cannons fired nothing but solid shot, heavy cast-iron balls. It was, in fact, the very weight of a cannon ball which determined the caliber of a gun. Thus, a "6-pounder" was not actually a piece weighing only an absurd six pounds, but rather a gun with a bore 3.67 inches in diameter which would fire a shot weighing six pounds and measuring 3.55 inches in diameter, the projectile always being slightly smaller than the gun bore, so that it could be rammed through it. These solid cannon balls, however, often rained harmlessly against the sides of a fortress, and so, a hollow round "shell" was devised which could be filled with powder and made to *explode* on the target at the moment of impact.

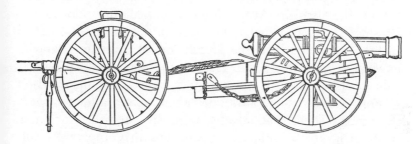

French 12-pounder, Napoleonic Wars

To do this required a "fuse" which the gunner could light just before ramming the ball down the muzzle. At first, these fuses were very crude, nothing but lengths of cord soaked in saltpeter. A gunner would "time" them, say, by reciting the Apostles' Creed while the projectile was in flight, and then apply corrections to subsequent rounds. These shells, often called "bombs" from the Latin *bombus* or booming sound, came to be effective and eventually in their more sophisticated form would doom wooden warships. In fact, in 1690 the British Admiralty actually refused to accept such a shell on the ground that it meant the end of navies, and Britain had the biggest navy to lose. Effective as shells became, however, they seemed an expensive weapon to be used against troops. One of them exploding among massed soldiery, of course, would do much harm—like the single Prussian shot that killed forty-two Russian soldiers at Zorndorf in 1758. But this was usually a lucky hit. If distant troops took cover or occupied the reverse slope of a hill, they were generally safe from cannon fire. Although case and grape were available, what was needed was *long-range* anti-personnel ammunition. Shrapnel supplied it when he devised a hollow cannon ball filled with small balls and a timed powder charge, which, upon exploding, would spray a distant area with projectiles.

He began his experiments in 1784, but it was twenty years before the British Army fully accepted the innovation. Shrapnel received its belated baptism of battle in 1804, when British troops attacked the Dutch fort at Surinam, Batavia, in what is now Indonesia. Here is the commander's report: "Shrapnel had so excellent an effect, as to cause the garrison of Fort Amsterdam to surrender at discretion after receiving the second shell. The enemy were so astonished at these shells as not to be able to account how they apparently suffered from musketry, at so great a distance as 2,050 yards." Thereafter shrapnel and all those variations of fragmenting anti-personnel shells which bear the same name became still another thorn in the bleeding flesh of the infantry.

Nevertheless, further development of artillery appears to have been stymied at this point, if only because a smooth spherical ball issuing from a smooth bore had a tendency to whirl and tumble in flight, thus losing much of its accuracy; and because the ball was smaller in diameter than the bore, the gases which it allowed to escape were not fully utilized, thus causing a loss in velocity. So it remained for the handgun to rescue its bigger brother from this dilemma.

The first handguns probably were the "cannon locks" (a "lock" is a gun's ignition system) of the fourteenth century. They were crude guns made by fixing a tube at the end of a pike or staff and firing it by pressing a lighted coal or hot iron over the touchhole at the end of the tube. The first true shoulder weapon, however, was the arquebus used so effectively by the Spanish infantry. This was the famous "matchlock" or "firelock," so called for the "slow match" made of

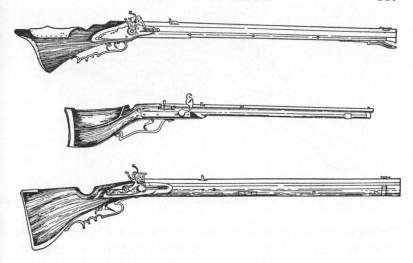

Arquebuses, Seventeenth Century

hemp and treated with saltpeter to make it slow burning. Held alongside the stock by a small C-shaped piece of metal, the firecord was pressed over the touchhole to ignite the powder charge in the barrel. The matchlock had its drawbacks, of course. For one thing, it could not be fired in wet weather, and for another the necessity of using one hand to manipulate the firecord made the piece difficult to aim. On the other hand, it lent itself to deception, and the Spanish sometimes frightened their opponents off at night by holding hundreds of firecords aloft to simulate a host of firelocks.

In the following century—the sixteenth—the wheel lock was introduced in Germany. The principle was a simple one still in use in today's cigarette lighters. A little serrated steel wheel spun against a flint sent a shower of sparks flashing down the touchhole. This was quickly followed by the flint-lock, a firing mechanism based upon a piece of flint striking a steel anvil to send sparks into the touchhole, and later, to send sparks into the grains of priming powder sprinkled into a pan. This simple change revolutionized firearms, and the

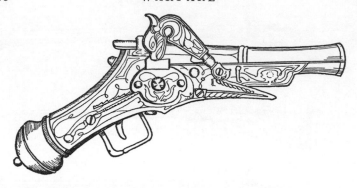

Wheel-lock Pistol

flintlock was for three centuries and more the chief weapon
of Europe and the Americas, the one which frightened Inca
and Iroquois alike. This in the main was the piece which the
Pilgrims brought to the New World, and it was with a flintlock
that Samuel de Champlain in 1609 began the wars of America when he employed one against the Iroquois on the shores
of the lake that bears his name. His own account of that encounter is illuminating: "I rested my musket against my cheek
and aimed directly at one of the three Chiefs. With the same
shot two fell to the ground; and one of their men was so
wounded that he died some time later. I had loaded my musket
with four balls."

It is revealing that Champlain uses the terms "arquebus"
and "musket" interchangeably, and it is likely that by then
the word "musket" was being used to describe all types of
shoulder weapons. It may have derived from the Italian word
moschetta, or "little hawk," perhaps given to one or another
of the various "locks" in the same fanciful way that gunsmiths would use Spanish words such as *aspide* or *drajón*
("asp" or "dragon") to christen their creations. Italy, of
course, being the most advanced and civilized area in the
world during the era of early firearms development, may well
have been the home of the handgun. Certainly the creative

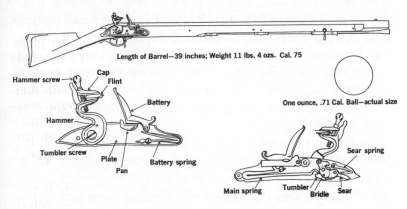

Length of Barrel—39 inches; Weight 11 lbs. 4 ozs. Cal. 75

One ounce, .71 Cal. Ball—actual size

British Flintlock—the Famous "Brown Bess"

geniuses of the Renaissance considered guns to be works of art. Both Leonardo da Vinci and Albrecht Dürer cast cannon, and the elaborate scrollwork and tracery on the stocks and barrels of medieval muskets and pistols will probably never be duplicated. Whatever its true source, the word "musket" came to be used to describe all forms of the infantry shoulder weapon which was the forerunner of today's rifle, and it received its last improvement in its ignition system with the development of the so-called "percussion lock" at the end of the eighteenth century.

Percussion depends upon an explosive which can be detonated by a sharp blow, a requirement filled by the discovery of fulminate of mercury around 1800. Seven years later a Scots Presbyterian minister named Alexander John Forsyth perfected a percussion priming powder which could be sprinkled on a priming pan above the touchhole and exploded by the blow of a hammer. In 1816, among other inventors, Thomas Shaw produced the percussion cap. Eventually this cap, usually made of copper, could be fixed upon a nipple or cone above the touchhole, and when it was struck by a direct blow from the hammer it fired the piece. With percussion caps, a musket could now be fired in windy or rainy weather. Thus, in 1841 a British general reported from the Far East: "A company of Sepoys, armed with flintlock muskets, which would not go off in a heavy rain, were closely surrounded by some 1,000 Chinese and were in imminent peril, when two companies of marines, armed with percussion-cap muskets, were ordered up, and soon dispersed the enemy with great loss."

As the art of musket-making progressed, however, it soon became apparent that it suffered from the same two defects which plagued artillery: the difficulties and dangers of loading at the muzzle, and the loss of effectiveness from smoothbore tubes. To solve these problems, two ideas emerged: loading at the breech or rear end of the barrel, and grooving the bore to seize a projectile and give it a spin that would improve its accuracy and range. Although both ideas were mutually supporting, the art of grooving or rifling (from the German *reifeln*, "to groove") developed first.

Gaspard Zoller of Vienna is said to have invented rifling about 1500 when he carved four straight grooves into the bore of his small arms. His purpose, however, was only for the grooves to receive the dirt accumulated from firing the piece and to allow air to escape so that the barrel would not burst. A few years later another German, Augustin Kutter of Nuremberg, used spiral grooves to propel a spinning musket ball. But it was not until 1742 that Benjamin Robins, an English mathematician with a penchant for artillery, laid down the principle that cylindrical projectiles fired through rifled bores were consistently more accurate than smoothbore round shot. Robins also warned that "whatever state shall thoroughly comprehend the nature and advantages of rifled barrel pieces" would dominate the battlefield.

Although the Industrial Revolution was just then beginning, gunsmiths still did not have the proper tools for rifling cannon, and so they turned to the smaller-caliber muskets in an effort to solve the problem. By the time of the Napoleonic Wars, the British and Germans had rifled muskets with which to oppose the French smoothbores. Although more accurate, they were still not satisfactory because the rifled musket was still a muzzle-loader. A man armed with it carried a belt full of paper "cartridges" containing both powder and ball. To fire his musket, he pulled a cartridge from his belt, bit off the end and sprinkled the firelock's pan with priming powder, after which he closed the pan, poured the rest of the powder down the barrel, rammed the ball and the paper down the barrel, withdrew the ramrod, took aim and pulled the trigger. If the flint sparked and the powder was dry, the musket would fire. With such a weapon, five rounds a minute was considered a rapid rate of fire, and only the most well-drilled troops could deliver sustained and accurate volleys of musketry. In fact, when Champlain spoke of "aiming" his piece at the Iroquois he meant that he was "pointing" it. The very flash and smoke of the priming powder before the charge fired would make aim difficult, and there never was a muzzle-loader equipped with a rear sight.

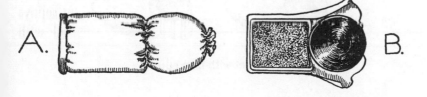

The First Cartridge: A. Paper Wrapper; B. Cross Section

Another defect of the rifled muzzle-loader was that it re-quired a ball small enough to be rammed home, and this small ball consequently allowed powder gases forming behind it to escape along the grooves. What was needed was a bullet which would expand into the grooves, to utilize the propellent force of the gases. This problem was solved in a most unexpected way. When on duty in Southern India a Captain Norton of the British Army examined native blowgun arrows and found that they had an elastic base which expanded against the inner surface of the pipe to prevent the escape of air past it. Using this idea, Norton in 1823 invented the first cylindro-conoidal bullet. It had a hollow base and when fired expanded into the rifling. Thirteen years later a London gunsmith named W. W. Greener improved on Norton's bullet by inserting a conoidal wooden plug into its base. And then, in 1849, the deadly Minié ball was produced by the French officer of that name. This was a conical bullet with an iron cup or plug at its base. When fired, the cup was thrust ahead into the bullet, expanding it against the rifling. There were other variations of the "expansive bullet," and one of them, the Pritchett, seems to have started a war. The famous Indian Mutiny or Sepoy Rebellion of 1853 is said to have begun when Moslem sepoys or soldiers refused to bite cartridges heavily smeared with unclean pork grease.

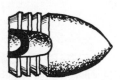 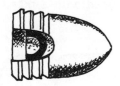

Minié bullet with iron cup

Minié bullet

There was one thing which all these expansive bullets had in common, however, and that was their great size. Varying from .702 to .54 caliber, they were monster bullets which could kill without necessarily striking a vital part. More important, they increased the effective killing range from 100 to 500 yards, and it is generally accepted as true that the use of the Minié ball by both sides in the American Civil War was chiefly responsible for the horrid loss of life in that conflict. Loss of limb, too, it might be added, for the only way in which the medicine of that day could cope with shattered extremities was to amputate them. No Civil War medical officer was ever without a good set of bone saws, and the fact is that the very word "sawbones" has flip-flopped into our dictionary as a derisive slang word for a physician. Moreover, many hands and forearms were mangled because the rifle of the time was still a muzzle-loader and a soldier had to expose at least his arm while loading it.

What was needed now was a "breech-loading" rifle which a marksman might load while lying prone, and this development occurred in 1841 when the Prussian Army issued its infantry the famous *Zündnadelgewehr*, or "needle gun," so called for its long and pointed firing pin. The needle gun was bolt-operated and its pin pierced a single paper cartridge containing percussion primer, powder and bullet. It could fire seven rounds a minute to the Minié's two, but more important than this it could be loaded while lying prone.

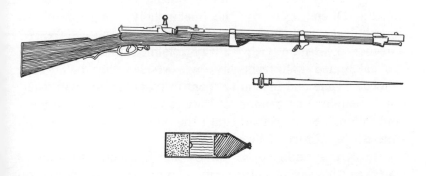

Prussian Needle Gun and Cartridge

Concurrently, as the problem of breech-loading was solved, the cannon makers had at last devised the tools to make the rifling of big guns practicable. They had not, however, been so fortunate in developing breech-loading artillery, if only because the various forms of breech blocks by which they sought to seal the rear of the cannon were always inadequate. The working parts either became clogged or warped, and frequently the force of the explosion either blew the block away or burst the barrel. So gunners were still compelled to run in front of their guns to load them at the muzzle, thus becoming more vulnerable to long-range rifle fire.

The superiority of breech-loading rifles over even rifled artillery was made dramatically clear in the Seven Weeks' War of 1866, when Prussia defeated Austria in the struggle for German leadership. At Königgrätz near what is now Sadowa in Czechoslovakia, the Austrian rifled artillery seemed to be dominating the Prussian muzzle-loaders, until Prussian infantry armed with needle guns delivered a surprise flanking attack on the Austrian right, shattering it with unprecedented small-arms fire.

Much as this spectacular victory for breech-loading small arms might emphasize the imperative need for breech-loading artillery, every attempt to devise satisfactory types ended in failure. Discouraged by the melancholy bang of blown breechblocks, ordnance experts despaired of success. W. W. Greener of Britain (who always claimed that Minié stole his celebrated ball from his own wooden-plug ball) concluded: "Time and ingenuity spent in planning and constructing breech-loading cannon will always end in disappointment and failure." So it seemed, until the ominous name of Krupp entered the history of firearms.

The Krupp family of Germany had been making guns as early as the seventeenth century, but in 1810 Napoleon Bonaparte's search for a Continental manufacturer of high-quality "British" steel led Friedrich Krupp to found the famous Krupp Works at Essen in 1810. It was in 1847, however, that his enterprising son, Alfred, forged the first link in the alliance between what was to become a dynasty of "Cannon Kings" and the spirit of Prussian militarism. In that year, Alfred Krupp presented the first artillery piece made in his new gunshop to King Frederick William of Prussia. A few years later, Krupp received an unprecedented order for 300 fieldpieces, and it was under the impetus of this contract that the Krupp Works had expanded by 1880 into a colossal complex comprising more than 500 iron mines, five huge steel plants, a steamship fleet, quarries, coal fields and clay pits, as well as the world's finest artillery proving ground complete with a private hotel for visiting buyers. By then, Krupp had developed a successful breech-loading artillery rifle. It was merely a block of steel sliding horizontally across the rear of a gun either to open or close it. The principle was one of pure mass. Thus, the breechblock on a 12-inch rifle weighed about a ton. But it worked. Krupp breech-loaders did not "blow," and there was hardly any leakage of powder gas. Armed with this superior artillery, as well as their superior rifles, the Germans had no difficulty subduing the French in the Franco-Prussian War of 1870–71.

When this conflict was followed by world-wide colonial competition for empire and for markets, the emphasis in gun-making shifted back to small arms. While eight European powers—Britain, France, Germany, Italy, Spain, Portugal, Belgium and Holland—within the space of a single genera- tion (1870–93) added 11,000,000 square miles of foreign land to their own rather modest total of 1,000,000 square miles, their rival armies sought to equip their soldiers with magazine rifles. This is merely a shoulder weapon fed by a "magazine" or supply chamber which enables a rifleman to fire five or six shots before reloading. It required a single metal cartridge which would be rigid enough to be stacked and held in place within the magazine and to be fed into the chamber by the bolt as it was pushed forward. Metal cartridges, especially those made of brass, also would expand upon firing and seal the chamber; and by cooling suddenly could be instantly ejected by the bolt as it was pulled backward. Obviously, magazine rifles conferred still greater firepower upon the ordinary foot soldier; and this power increased further through the development of machine guns.

The idea of machine guns or multiple-fire small arms seems to be nearly as old as firearms themselves. Probably the first successful form, however, was the American Gatling gun, introduced toward the end of the Civil War by a reluctant Abraham Lincoln and used effectively at San Juan Hill in the Spanish-American War. But the multiple-barrel Gatling, of course, along with many of its imitators, was operated by a crank. It remained for the American-born Sir Hiram S. Maxim to develop a machine gun operated by the force of its own recoil. In 1884, he patented the deadly Maxim gun, a one-barrel weapon weighing only forty pounds but capable of firing 2,000 rounds in three minutes. With the Maxim, infantry firepower became formidable indeed. Its range rivaled that of the artillery, an advantage which was obviated by universal adoption of rifled cannon.

Artillery was revolutionized again in 1867, when Alfred Nobel, a Swedish scientist more famous for having created the Nobel Peace Prize, perfected a stable form of high explosive which he called "dynamite." Shells packed with dynamite could now be fired to explode upon impact, or at any moment which the developing marvels of timed ammunition might designate. Thus, chiefly through the efforts of this lover of peace and abhorrer of war, the art of maiming and killing became ever more efficient. A few decades later, the centuries-old dream of "smokeless" powder was realized by a French chemist named Vieille. Up until 1886, the "smoke of battle," which is today generally a figure of speech, was a choking, swirling, pungent reality. Black-powder smoke from small arms as well as artillery could within a few hours of combat raise clouds that literally blotted out the sun. Moreover, black-powder smoke gave away a gun's position, as it did with the Americans firing their archaic ammunition at San Juan. After the development of smokeless powder, however, and up until the development of flash-and-explosion detection systems, artillery could generally depend upon concealment.

At about this time also the universal adoption of elongated or cylindrical shells as distinct from the old spherical shells had caused considerable confusion in nomenclature. The old method of measuring guns by pounds from the weight of the shell it fired was no longer adequate. This was because elongated shells were heavier than spherical ones. Thus, a 12-inch cast-iron round shot weighed about 230 pounds, while an elongated shell 12 inches in diameter weighed 700 pounds. Obviously, it was ridiculous to call the U.S. 12-inch rifle of 1874 a "700-pounder." So it became known as a "12-incher," and cannon once classified by the weight of the shell they fired were now catalogued by the diameter of their gun bore. Gradually, for some vague reason, perhaps the fact that field artillery was developed in Europe with its metric system of measurement, and naval rifles developed in Britain with its linear measure, ground ordnance came to be measured in "millimeters" and naval artillery in "inches." Thus, to speak of the "16-inchers" mounted by the mighty battleship *New Jersey* is not to speak of some ridiculously puny gun 16 inches in length, but one with a bore 16 inches in diameter and firing a projectile weighing 1,800 pounds. When transposing the millimeters of field artillery into naval inches, or vice versa, the handiest rule of thumb is that 25 millimeters are roughly the equivalent of an inch, and that the famous French 75-millimeter gun of World War I would measure 2.95 inches.

The French seventy-five represented the "cannon-cocker's"

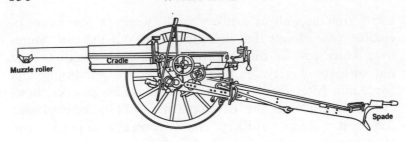

French 75-mm Field Gun

final triumph over the mechanical harpie that had haunted him since the inception of artillery: the problem of recoil. A soldier's shoulder might absorb the recoil of his musket or rifle, but there was nothing on earth as yet to prevent a big gun from leaping backward when fired. And when a gun's recoil forced it backward, the gunners were obliged to drag it forward again to "re-lay" or re-sight it. Such exertion could be most wearying, especially under the conditions of prolonged battle. At Waterloo in 1815, the gunners in a British battery of 9-pounders became so exhausted from hauling and rehauling their recoiled guns forward that they began to fire from the recoiled position, falling farther and farther back with each discharge until they were at last on the edge of their own artillery park, where the slightest accident could have exploded their ammunition wagons and torn a serious hole in Wellington's line.

Secondly, although the development of breech-loading guns had spared cannoneers the danger of running forward to load their guns at the muzzle, the improved range and accuracy of small arms had presented a new peril. Either artillery stayed out of rifle range and thereby out of sight of its targets, or else the gunners risked the wrath of sniper fire. Artillerists often fired their piece from the brow of the hill, hoping that its recoil would carry it out of sight where it might be reloaded in safety. Even so, by having to run it forward again and re-sight it, the gunner gained no advantage from accuracy on his first round. Each shot had to be sighted individually and there was no hope of pouring a concentrated fire into a target hit or nearly hit on the opening rounds.

By mastering the problem of recoil, therefore, a gun could be made to fire more rapidly and more accurately. Shock absorption was the answer, of course, and by 1870 the American munition-maker Benjamin B. Hotchkiss had already opened European plants to manufacture quick-firing guns in calibers as high as 57 millimeters. By 1884 the British Navy had perfected similar pieces as big as 4.7 inches which could fire ten rounds in forty-seven seconds. Naval artillery, however, has always possessed the advantage of being fired from a fairly stable platform. Merely to see a battleship is to understand that there is nothing on land quite so solid, but field artillery pieces mounted on carriages seemed by their very nature to be prone to recoil.

So the armies and the gunsmiths of Europe began their scramble to be the first to perfect the "dream gun" that would remain stationary while firing. They resorted to all sorts of devices, most of which were, in effect, "recoil brakes"—and it was such a device that Captain Alfred Dreyfus was falsely accused of having betrayed to the Germans. In the end, chiefly through the untiring efforts of Colonel Hippolyte Langlois, the French won the race. They produced the marvelous, quick-firing 75 millimeter cannon based upon a non-recoiling carriage and equipped with a bulletproof shield to protect its gunners. Artillery experts were astonished to learn that the seventy-five actually had *seats* on it for gunners to occupy when it fired. It was so stationary when discharged that a glass of water placed upon the rim of one of its wheels did not spill a drop. Its rate of fire was at first twenty rounds per minute, and then, with perfection of semi-automatic action by which the exploding gases opened the breech and ejected the cartridge, the rate rose to thirty per minute.

Eventually, of course, larger calibers were equipped with

recoilless carriages; and thus it was through the invention of the French seventy-five, the world's first quick-firing gun, that the earth of Europe was to be soaked in blood during World War I. Rapid-firing artillery backing up machine guns, magazine rifles and barbed wire was to strengthen the defense, stop the offense and stabilize the battlefield in a bloody bind.

From the development of recoilless, quick-firing guns, a difference in the kind of artillery, it was only a step to the design and production of bigger and bigger pieces differing only in size and destructive power. Thus, in World War I the Germans fielded monster howitzers, among them the famous Big Bertha, a 16.5 inch mammoth capable of hurling an 1,800-pound shell a distance of nine miles. A Belgian statesman who saw a Big Bertha being dragged through Liège described his feelings upon seeing it:

The monster advanced in two parts, pulled by thirty-six horses. The pavement trembled. The crowd remained mute with consternation at the appearance of this phenomenal apparatus. . . . Hannibal's elephants could not have astonished the Romans more! The soldiers who accompanied it marched stiffly with an almost religious solemnity. It was the Belial of cannons! In the Parc D'Avroy it was carefully mounted and scrupulously aimed. Then came the frightful explosion. The crowd was flung back, the earth shook like an earthquake and all the windowpanes in the vicinity were shattered. . . .

After World War I, there were no basic or revolutionizing changes in guns. True, the fusing of firearms onto the internal combustion engines which produced tanks* and military aircraft was a far-reaching innovation, but the effect was

---

* The "tank" got its name from the secrecy with which the British sought to enshroud Winston Churchill's proposed development of this "land battleship." At first, the vehicle was called a "water carrier," and this was abbreviated to "W.C." But "W.C." is also an abbreviation of the British water closet or toilet, and so, when some indignant British officers balked at serving on "the W.C. Commission," the name was changed to "water tank," and thence shortened to tank.

German 28-cm (11-Inch) Siege Gun, World War I

upon mobility, upon the means of advancing guns and bombs either across or above the battlefield, not upon the guns and shells themselves. During World War II the only true changes in weaponry were the use of rockets, aerial bombs delivered by the force of gravity and the development of the A-bomb. Otherwise, weaponry was refined rather than changed, chiefly through improvements in radio and electronics.

A flamethrower discharging flame through a tube was still operating on the principle of a gun, and even napalm bombs —though dropped from aircraft—were a variation either on the Greek fire of the medievals or the heated shot and "carcasses," that is, hollow, perforated balls filled with pitch, with which the British set Charlestown, Massachusetts, afire during the Revolution. Small arms have by all means grown more prolific since 1914–18, so that the ordinary American foot soldier fighting the guerrilla war of Vietnam is now armed with an M-16 rifle firing lightweight .22 caliber ammunition at the incredible rate of up to 120 rounds per minute. But this, nevertheless, is only a refinement of earlier automatic and semi-automatic weapons. The hand grenade so vital to guerrilla warfare, although packed with explosive and fragmented to explode à la shrapnel, is actually nothing more than a variant of the stones which our ancestors hurled at each other; and which our descendants may again employ, should we fail to curb our collective tempers. It is also true that artillery has grown longer in range, more accurate and more powerful in explosion and penetration. But this too is an increase, not a change such as rifling or breech-loading.

After tanks and aircraft appeared; artillery was compelled to develop the specialties of antitank and anti-aircraft ordnance; but these also, except for the self-propelled rockets used now in missile weaponry, were guns. It is again true that timing devices have become marvelously refined. Any GI who fought in Hürtgen Forest during World War II will not forget the "tree-bursts" of the German artillery, and many an enemy aircraft was downed by the American radio proximity fuse which detonated any shell merely passing near the target. Certainly, the various forms of explosives proliferated, among them the "plastic" types which, so suitable to the uses of sabotage or guerrilla warfare, may be molded into any shape to fit any receptacle, or even merely stuck to the target like a wad of gum.

In chemical and biological warfare, to poison the enemy with gas or infect him with microbes, it is still necessary to fire these dreadful canisters from a gun or drop them from an airplane or spray them through a tube which is only another variation of a gun. Smoke, phosphorus, flares and thermal substances all are borne in bomb or shell. To describe or detail the development of any or all of them would not be germane to this study.

What is vitally relevant, however, is the invention of

nuclear weapons. Here firearms are left behind and war is given a new and hideous dimension. The difference is vast enough to be one of kind rather than degree. And yet, so much is known about the development of ultimate weapons that this study, once again, will not be served by describing it. What matters most of all, it would seem, is that the weapons of war appear in the main to have been the product of the labors of men of peace. Scientists and scholars, men of mind and conscience who abhor bloodshed, have willingly or unwillingly placed the gift of their inventions in the hands of "men of blood."

It was gold, not guns, that beguiled the monk Berthold Schwarz; it was peace, not war, that remained the paramount purpose of Nobel, the inventor of dynamite; and although the inquiries of Albert Einstein were certainly not directed toward producing mushroom clouds, that was how they ended. Realizing this, one cannot help recalling the question asked by Carlyle one full century ago: "The first ground handful of nitre, sulphur and charcoal drove monk Schwarz's pestle through the ceiling: what will the last do?"

10. DOWN TO THE SEA IN SHIPS

If the idea of an army seems to be as old as civilization, so too does the notion of a navy. Apparently, men have been striking each other at sea almost from the inception of boats and ships, be they the inflated animal skins or hollowed-out tree trunks of the primitives or our own nuclear-powered submarines and aircraft carriers. And the fact is that just as the recorded history of warfare seems to date from the fifteenth century B.C., when Thutmose III of Egypt defeated the Syrians at Megiddo (Biblical Armageddon), so too do the annals of sea operations. That same Thutmose maintained a fleet of ships to transport troops for his Syrian campaigns, seizing and utilizing Phoenician harbors to maintain a flow of supplies and men just as General Eisenhower did in his invasion of Europe.

But if it may also be said of navies that the more they change the more they are the same thing, there does seem to be one distinction: not until the sixteenth century of the Christian era, when the sea powers of Europe became locked in the colonial struggle finally won by Britain, was there such a thing as a "warship." Up until then, all ships looked alike, and a sailing vessel was a ship of war or peace only according to the intentions of those aboard her. Actually, the earliest concept of a sea fight considered the ship itself as hardly more than a seaworthy platform from which archers and spearmen —the earliest marines—might shoot at one another. Ships did not fight ships until the oared galleys of the ancient world were equipped with beaks mounted on the prow for the purpose of ramming. Vessels also were fitted with a storming bridge from which boarding parties might pour onto the decks of a rammed ship or one brought alongside by a wide variety of grappling hooks. Although these long and graceful galleys were also equipped with masts and sails, they usually lowered them for battle, fearing to risk the instability of a head wind.

Once these ramming and boarding tactics had supplanted what Thucydides derided as "the somewhat old-fashioned kind" of fighting whereby the rival marines fought a pitched battle from the decks of motionless ships, success at sea came to depend more on a skipper's ability to maneuver his vessel and his crew's capacity to carry out his orders. It might even be said that when this happened the tactics of mass and maneuver were also adopted at sea. Certainly the rival fleets fought each other with means remarkably similar to the "three points of a line" concept still dominating land warfare.

They also arranged their forces in a "line." Sometimes they sought a penetration or breakthrough whereby all the galleys dashed forward on a sudden signal to pierce the enemy line, after which they wheeled right and left to strike his unguarded rear. There were also flanking attacks aiming at turning either extremity for the same objective of taking the enemy in the rear. Defensively, a fleet might counter a breakthrough by forming its vessels into a hedgehog, that is, in a circle with bows pointing outward and sterns to the rear, as the Greeks did against the Persians at Artemisium in 480 B.C. Or they might construct a floating fort by lashing their big ships together with cables, à la the Venetians against the Normans 1,562 years later. Like a general on land, an admiral might ward off a flanking attack by extending his line in the threatened direction; or, if he were fighting in landlocked waters, by anchoring one flank of his own line on the shore. A fleet with superior numbers might advance in two lines, so that the second one could handle any enemy ships breaking through the first.

Numerical superiority could be countered by drawing the stronger force into narrow waters where the ships would become jammed together in confusion. This was what the Greeks under Themistocles did to the Persians under Xerxes in the great naval battle of Salamis in 480 B.C. The Greek playwright Aeschylus, who fought at Salamis as a marine, has left a stirring account of the battle. In his *Persae,* a Persian messenger announcing the defeat to the mother of Xerxes declares:

> The first rammer was a Greek
> Which sheared away a great Sidonian's crest;
> Then close, one on another, charged the rest.
> At first the long-drawn Persian line was strong
> And held; but in those narrows such a throng
> Was crowded, a ship to ship could bring no aid.
> Nay, with their own bronze-fanged beaks they made
> Destruction; a whole length of oars one beak
> Would shatter; and with purposed art the Greek
> Ringed us outside, and pressed, and struck; and we—
> Our oarless hulls went over, till the sea
> Could scarce be seen, with wrecks and corpses spread.*

Few accounts of naval tactics could be more lucid or poetic, and Salamis, of course, remains one of the great sea fights of all time. It is safe to accord it the same judgment which Sir Edward Creasy makes on Marathon, the land battle it made possible ten years later: "It secured for mankind the intellectual treasures of Athens, the growth of free institutions, the liberal enlightenment of the western world and the gradual ascendancy for many ages of the great principles of European civilization."

Naval tactics did not vary appreciably after Salamis. In fact, they remained static for the next 2,000 years, waiting, like ground warfare, to be revolutionized by the discovery of gunpowder and the voyages of discovery. It may even be

* Gilbert Murray translation.

said that the concept of a navy as it is held today is a distinctly modern idea which could not emerge until sails replaced oars as the main means of nautical propulsion. There were, of course, "navies" of a sort in the era of Historic Warfare. Thucydides seems to think that "Minos," or whomever it was that ruled the Minoan civilization based on Crete, organized the first navy around 1500 B.C. Probably, it was a fleet intended to put down piracy and protect Minoan trading ships.

Ancient Galley

The Phoenicians, who dominated the eastern Mediterranean for three centuries, founding the great colony of Carthage in 800 B.C. near the site of modern Tunis, were a seagoing people who certainly required sea power to protect their trading ships. So too did the Greeks who swarmed over the Mediterranean like water bugs on a pond, and it has been suggested that the siege of Troy was not begun by Agamem-

non to recover the wife of his brother Menelaus, but rather
was part of an overall struggle for sea supremacy in the
Aegean. When emergent Rome collided with Carthage, she,
too, found that she needed a navy; and with characteristic
clear-sightedness she swallowed her aversion to salt water and
built an all-conquering fleet. In fact, the great naval Battle of
Actium in 31 B.C. at which Augustus defeated the forces of
Marc Antony to become the first of the Roman emperors,
was won with a Roman navy. There were, of course, medieval
navies such as the Venetian, Spanish, or Turkish. The very
word "admiral" is, in fact, derived from the Arabic *amir-al-
bahr*, commander of the sea. And in the centuries of conflict
between Islam and Christendom, no confrontation on land
was more momentous than the Battle of Lepanto (1571) at
which the Christian fleet under Don John of Austria defeated
the Moslem Turks under Ali Pasha. Here was a sea battle that
shattered the myth of Turkish invincibility and liberated
Europe from a century of terror. It was, perhaps, the last
glory of a Christendom in division and dissolution, and it has
been immortalized by G. K. Chesterton's stirringly evocative
ode to Don John, "the last of the troubadours."

In that enormous silence, tiny and unafraid,
Comes⁻ up along a winding road the noise of the Crusade.
Strong gongs groaning as the guns boom far,
Don John of Austria is going to the war;
Stiff flags straining in the night-blasts cold
In the gloom black-purple, in the glint old-gold,
Torchlight crimson on the copper kettle-drums,
Then the tuckets, then the trumpets, then the cannon, and he comes.

Nevertheless, for all these fleets and sea fights, the modern
concept of navies and sea power was the result of the same
revolutions in firearms and navigation which ushered in the
era of Modern Warfare on land. True enough, there were
guns at Lepanto, and for two centuries before that; but the
tactics were the old close-fighting, ramming tactics of the
inland seas.

There was as yet no notion of a navy in the permanent sense of a fleet always in being. Kings still would hire ships from private contractors, or, in the English way, meet a particular crisis with a particular fleet which could be raised by ordering a muster of ships at the Tower of London. There, the trading vessel would be made into a warship by the addition of "castles" built fore and aft as fighting platforms for soldiers. Today, one thinks of a navy as a nation's *permanent* striking force at sea. Its purpose is to continue in a state of readiness for war; and when war comes, to control the seas, or at least those waters adjacent to the theater of war, either by the destruction or intimidation of the rival sea power. Controlling the sea, a navy may supply and reinforce the ground forces, may land them on the enemy coast, may give them gunfire or aerial support, may exhaust the enemy by a blockade or destroy his ground forces by intercepting them at sea. Although this, apart from gunfire and aerial support, was certainly understood by the ancients, the concept of a standing navy was foreign to them. This was because their world was still limited. Once the entire globe had been opened up to the enterprise of ships driven by wind alone and capable of long voyages, so too did the world become an arena for the competition of sea powers. That competition, based upon the notion that one's empire and sovereignty might be stretched as far as one's ships might sail, naturally led to the development of true "navies."

Neither of these concepts was immediately grasped, but were perceived only gradually, dawningly, as the possibilities inherent in a true *warship*—and by extension, a true navy— became clearer to the competing nations of Europe. Probably, it is no exaggeration to say that this did not occur until a long century after King Henry VIII of England produced the first fighting ship. Traditionally, this is said to be in 1513 when he had gun ports cut along the broadside of the *Mary Rose.* Before this, guns had been mounted all over a ship, and they generally were fired by soldiers or marines while the ship's skipper and sailors merely busied themselves with sailing. After this, however, the ominous line of gun ports stretching fore and aft along both sides of a vessel clearly identified her as a warship. Moreover, the seamen now "fought" as well as sailed their ships, and as the soldiers returned to land, only coming aboard as passengers or marines, the word "sailor" came to mean a professional sea warrior as distinct from a "merchant mariner." Finally, the warship or man-of-war ended the era of close fighting and led to the concept of a sea fight as a gun duel.

This innovation was almost entirely due to the British, who placed great emphasis on the naval gun as a ship-killer, while the French and Spanish, particularly the latter, required more time to discard the nobleman's foolish prejudice against cowardly firearms. A second British concept was to give them another advantage over their Franco-Spanish rivals. This was the tactical principle of firing low to destroy the enemy's ship. Thus, British broadsides were fired on the downward roll of the waves with the intention of piercing the hull to sink or disable the ship, or at least to subject enemy crewmen to showers of wooden splinters. The Spanish and French preferred to fire on the upward roll with the intent of ruining the masts and rigging and thus destroying the ship's motive power. To the British, then, the object was to "kill" ships with gunfire, and the notion of taking one captive was only secondary; to the Franco-Spanish the paramount purpose was to cripple a ship, which could then be boarded and captured. In fact, the rival tactics were succinctly summarized by the instructions King Philip II issued to the Spanish Armada before it sailed to invade England in 1588.

"The enemy's object," Philip wrote, "will be to fight at long distance in consequence of his advantage in artillery. . . . The aim of our men . . . must be to bring him to close quarters and grapple with him." To this end, Philip loaded his ships with soldiers until he had an 18 to 1 advantage. In the event,

Spanish Galleon, Sixteenth Century

British tactics triumphed, and the defeat of the Armada during that momentous six days of battle in the English Channel
marks a turning point in the evolution of sea fighting. With
an assist from the weather, the British fleet's superiority in
seamanship, gunnery and naval tactics shattered Philip's
dream of conquering England.

Meanwhile, as the Spanish threat receded, the energetic
Cardinal Richelieu in France perceived the value of a standing navy and proceeded to build one during the second
quarter of the seventeenth century, thus opening the second
round of European naval rivalry and giving the British one
more shove toward inception of a standing navy. In 1634,
King Charles I introduced the abhorred tax known as "ship

money" for the purpose of constructing a navy "which is very needful, for the French have prepared a fleet, and challenge a dominion in the seas, where anciently they durst not fish for gurnets without a license."

Although the French threat faded with the death of Richelieu, a new rivalry rose when, in the last half of the century, the seven northern provinces of the Spanish Netherlands successfully rebelled, becoming known as the United Provinces and ultimately, under the leadership of the province of Holland, as the Dutch Republic. It was only natural that the seagoing Dutch should build a navy—Europe's fourth major fleet—and enter the growing competition for colonies and dominion of the seas. Inevitably, Holland challenged Britain and became her enemy. There followed the three Anglo-Dutch Wars, all naval struggles, and when the last one was over in 1674, Britain was again triumphant.

During this struggle, the British refined their technique of naval fighting. Against the Armada they had already begun to attack in "line-ahead" formation, that is, one ship following the other so that all of a fleet's ships might fire broadside on one target at the same time. This tactic superseded the old "line-abreast" whereby a fleet attacked in a kind of naval phalanx. Obviously, the line-abreast tactic was suitable to ships massing with the intent to ram and break through the enemy line; but it became self-defeating for gunships firing broadsides. Although the line-ahead tactic became universal, the British formalized it by specifying that each ship must sail 100 yards apart from the other. Gradually, of course, there were departures from this rigorist naval doctrine, which appeared to presume that the enemy would acquiesce in his foreordained role of placing his leading ship exactly opposite the British leader and so on down the line. In its defense, however, it must be pointed out that in those days communications between ships at sea were very faulty indeed. A man's voice even when issuing from a speaking trumpet rarely carried more than a dozen yards or so across wind-whipped water, and with no system of flag-signaling yet developed a commander could only direct his scattered ships by the imperfect and unreliable means of signal guns. Therefore, an admiral usually issued his orders before the battle, and since they could not be rapidly altered, they had to remain fairly rigid. Even so, one variation on the line-ahead was the "melee" whereby control would pass from the admiral to individual commanders eager to exploit immediate advantages or escape adverse ones. A melee sometimes became a ship-for-ship, shot-for-shot struggle. Even if the fleet commander was a rigorist, once the enemy had been put to flight he would generally order a chase from which a melee would ensue. Yet, as much as the rival schools of naval tactics might differ, the British at least never veered from their policy of putting to sea to attack and destroy the enemy. Because of this, they almost always sought the "weather gauge" of battle.

To hold the weather gauge is to have the advantage of the wind so that one might steer directly for the enemy. Its opposite is the "leeward gauge," and the two phrases summarize opposing schools of naval doctrine comparable to the ideas of offense and defense. The weather gauge is the offensive spirit, because to "be to windward" is to have the power of giving or refusing battle. With the wind in one's sails, one may or may not attack. The defects of this virtue are, naturally enough, the advantages of holding the lee-gauge. Attack entails exposure, irregularity and the sacrifice of firepower incurred in approaching the enemy. And the fleet on the lee, although it has lost the initiative, may remain orderly while subjecting the exposed assailant to concentrated gunfire. In another way, to hold the weather gauge was to hold the advantage of speed or mobility, and it may be said that once sails were supplanted by steam, the speediest fleet was the one holding the "weather gauge."

Thus, during the centuries now known as the "age of fighting sail," the British, always wishing to attack and destroy, customarily sought the weather gauge. The French, desiring to preserve ships and even avoid battle while crippling the approaching enemy, usually maneuvered for the lee gauge. The British, then, were offensive-minded at sea and the French defensive-minded, a fact which was to emerge with startling clarity once Louis XIV of France challenged Britain to the second round of Anglo-French naval warfare lasting from 1689 to 1713. By then, of course, the sailing warship was supreme on the sea, so much so that in 1684 a single French man-of-war was able to defeat thirty-five galleys. By then also all the sea powers had adopted the custom of "rating" their ships in categories ranging from a "first-rate" man-of-war mounting 100 or more guns through a second-rater of 80 guns to a sixth-rater of 18. Usually, the true "capital ship" was a vessel mounting between 70 and 140 guns. Gradually, however, as it became plain that the top-raters were too expensive to build, they were abandoned in favor of lower-raters which were in turn made larger. Eventually the true capital ship was the 74-gun man-of-war which, with some smaller ships mounting as few as 54 guns, came to be known as "ships-of-the-line-of-battle" or "line-of-battle-ships." It is from these phrases that the modern term "battleship" was born midway in the nineteenth century. It meant the largest or capital *gunfire* ships of a fleet. Although the modern aircraft carrier is now indubitably larger than a battleship, its primary purpose is not to deliver aimed gunfire.

So it was with these line-of-battle-ships that the British and French fought again for supremacy of the sea, and when the Treaty of Utrecht ended the War of the Spanish Succession in 1713, it was Britain who emerged as history's first queen of the waves. She had driven both France and Spain from the ocean, and had so used her Dutch allies that though they were triumphant on land they were exhausted at sea. As Mahan writes, ". . . she was *the* sea power, without any

Early Ship of the Line

second. This power also she held alone, unshared by friend and unchecked by foe." Becoming the first true sea power, Britain felt a need for overseas bases so that her ships, in effect, might patrol the world. Understanding this, she insisted that Spain cede her the mighty naval base of Gibraltar commanding the narrow waters between the Atlantic and the Mediterranean. She sought more bases when the Seven Years' War (1756–1763) opened the third round of the Anglo-French sea struggle.

By then line-of-battle-ships had become so standardized in design that it was often impossible to tell the ships of one fleet from the other. In fact, sailing under false colors was such an established *ruse de guerre* that ships always carried a set of enemy flags in their lockers. In 1759, when a British

Early Frigate

fleet carried James Wolfe's army up the St. Lawrence to Quebec, some of its ships flew the lily-flag of France in order to lure unsuspecting river pilots on board. During this war also a new kind of fighting ship appeared: the frigate. Speedy and seaworthy, usually a sixth-rater mounting 28 or 30 guns, the frigate was to be used as a scouting ship and to become the "eyes of the fleet." Gradually, frigates came to mount more guns and to be used as fighting ships as well as scouts and couriers. During the War of 1812 the American 44-gun *Constitution,* better known as *Old Ironsides,* was one of a class of fast, well-armed frigates. That struggle, even more than the Revolution, was the true birth throes of the United States Navy. More than the exploits of Fighting Jack Barry or of John Paul Jones, the single-ship victories of Isaac Hull in *Constitution* or Stephen Decatur in her sister ship *United States,* as well as James Lawrence's immortal death cry "Don't give up the ship," Oliver Hazard Perry's signal triumph on Lake Erie and Macdonough's decisive defeat of the British on

Lake Champlain, thrilled a nation sick of an indigestible diet of retreat and defeat on land. So thoroughly did the upstart Yankee skippers twist the tail of the British sea lions that even the *Times* of London was led to lament: "What is wrong with British sea power?" And although the *Bonhomme Richard* is surely and justly famous in American naval lore, no schoolboy has forgotten Oliver Wendell Holmes's stirring tribute to *Old Ironsides:*

> Nail to the mast her holy flag,
> Set every threadbare sail,
> And give her to the god of storms,
> The lightning and the gale!

The War of 1812, incidentally, was part of the final round of the Anglo-French struggle for colonial and maritime supremacy, the period of the Revolutionary–Napoleonic Wars stretching from 1793 to 1815. Once again, sea power was to be decisive, and the climactic battle was fought off Cape Trafalgar on the southwest coast of Spain in 1805. Trafalgar stands as probably the most famous naval battle of all time, and the victor is perhaps also the most famous admiral: Horatio Nelson of Britain. Lord Nelson not only conquered at Trafalgar and the Nile and elsewhere, he reopened naval tactics. It was his genius to grant subordinates the opportunity to act on their own initiative, always presuming that they were thoroughly imbued with his own credo of "close and decisive battle." And they were so inspired, having gone into history as a "band of brothers" who sometimes wept when Nelson stood among them to outline his audacious plans. At Trafalgar, Nelson attacked the Franco-Spanish fleet under Villeneuve in two lines: one commanded by the faithful Collingwood, the other by himself. His plan was to strike the enemy's vanguard and center while Collingwood attacked the rear. In essence, that was what happened, although Nelson did not survive to celebrate his greatest victory.

Trafalgar shattered Napoleon's dream of invading Britain, forced him back onto his Continental System and that unequal economic war with Britain which he had no chance of winning and led ultimately to the field at Waterloo. If Waterloo, the most famous and one of the most decisive land battles, was a result of Trafalgar, and it was, then Trafalgar was *the* decisive battle of the Napoleonic Wars. When it was over, Britain's dominion of the seas was unchallenged, and she was able to enforce that *Pax Britannica* which kept the peace of Europe for a hundred years.

Although Trafalgar did not introduce any special innovations in naval warfare, if one excepts Nelson's highly flexible audacity and improvements in flag-signaling and gunnery, especially among the highly-trained British crews, it was nevertheless the end of the age of fighting sail. Between Trafalgar and the Spanish-American naval battles of 1898 lies nearly a century in which there are no more great sea fights between ships-of-the-line; and yet, just because it is in this period that the battleship sheds her sails and then changes her shape, the developments in ship construction and the appearance of new vessels and weapons make a fascinating chapter in the annals of seagoing arms.

In 1855 the first mines were used when the Russians sowed the Baltic sea lanes with floating canisters of explosives. They were cone-shaped containers made of zinc, two feet deep and eighteen inches wide, packed with gunpowder and detonated by glass tubes filled with acid which broke on contact with a ship's hull. Originally, mines were called "torpedoes," and this is the explanation of Farragut's seemingly anachronistic "Damn the torpedoes!" at Mobile Bay. There were, of course, no true locomotive torpedoes in 1864. But there were two years later, after Captain Luppis of the Austrian Navy and a Scottish engineer named Robert Whitehead developed an elongated "explosion vessel" which traveled underwater and was therefore completely invisible. Propelled by compressed air, it was able to move under its own power.

The first torpedoes were fired from boats equipped with launching tubes. When these crude predecessors of the PT boats of World War II began to become effective ship-killers, naval architects busied themselves designing "torpedo-boat destroyers." Equipped with light guns and torpedo tubes of their own, these sleek, speedy vessels soon came to be called "destroyers." In order of size and armament, they ranked just a little behind a frigate. Gradually, the destroyer proved itself to be capable of carrying out an even greater variety of missions than the frigate; and when the torpedo-launching submarine appeared and the destroyer turned from destroying torpedo-boats to killing undersea craft, she all but made her older, larger sister obsolete.

Submarines, of course, were almost an exclusively American innovation. Robert Fulton and David Bushnell are its true parents. In 1776 during the Revolution, Bushnell's prototype submarine very nearly sank Admiral Sir Richard Howe's flagship, *Eagle*. Even as it is done today, this one-man vessel submerged or surfaced by flooding its bilges or emptying them out. It was driven by a screw propeller operated by a hand crank, and its charge was a container filled with 150 pounds of gunpowder carried on the outside. This was released by withdrawing a bolt which primed a time detonator, after which the submarine turned and fled. In its attack on *Eagle,* the Bushnell submarine failed because its untrained operator gave himself away by repeated surfacing, and was thus forced to release his charge prematurely. Twenty-one years later, Robert Fulton's *Nautilus* successfully blew up a French schooner during a trial experiment off the French coast. But it remained for the American Civil War to produce the first recorded instance of a warship sunk by a submarine. In 1864 the thirty-foot, eight-man Confederate submarine *H. L. Hunley* torpedoed and sank the Federal ship *Housatonic,* and went down with her.

With that event, the age of submarine warfare began; so that the undersea vessel, rejected at first by the French and

then by the British as too terrible to use, only to be developed
by the Americans and seized upon by the Germans, became
the chief killer of commerce and enemy warships in both
World Wars and is now perhaps, what with nuclear-powered
submarines able to circumnavigate the world submerged or to
fire nuclear missiles from the depths of the sea, the modern
navy's vessel of the future.

German Submarine, World War I

From that American Civil War which produced not only
the first successful submarine attack, but so many other
"firsts" in land weaponry and tactics as well, there came also
that first momentous battle between steam-propelled ironclads, the historic standoff between *Monitor* and *Merrimac*
at Hampton Roads in 1862. This was the first battle between
"battleships" in the modern sense, and it climaxed a period of
ship and gun development begun as far back as 1807 when
Robert Fulton launched the first commercially feasible steamship. This "monster moving on the waters, defying the winds
and tide and breathing flames and smoke," this steamship
christened *Clermont* and derided as "Fulton's Folly" was to
revolutionize the maritime world and by extension naval
warfare.

In fact, it was Fulton who also built the first steam warship, the *Demologos,* renamed the *Fulton,* launched in 1814. Intended for defense of New York in the War of 1812, *Demologos* was a twin-hulled paddle-wheeler with one hull housing the engines, the other the boiler, and with the paddle wheel in between. She mounted thirty 32-pounder guns, and also had submarine guns firing 100-pound projectiles from beneath the water-line. What *Demologos* might have done to the sailing warships of that time remains a subject for useless speculation, because the war ended before she could enter battle.

For the next few decades, steam-powered warships were variants of Fulton's paddle-wheelers, and in fact the steamships which supported Winfield Scott in his amphibious operation against Vera Cruz during the Mexican War were also paddle-wheelers. It remained for the development of the screw propeller to rid the steamship of its unlovely paddle, and thus, to streamline warships. Exactly who was first to perfect a workable screw propeller is difficult to say, although it appears that one patented in 1836 by the Swedish-born American designer John Ericsson may be entitled to that distinction. In 1843, the ten-gun sloop *Princeton* was equipped with a six-bladed Ericsson screw propeller; *Princeton* could do an astonishing 13 knots.* Unfortunately, one of her guns blew up, killing the U.S. Secretary of State and Secretary of the Navy, who were aboard for her trials, as well as members of the crew. For a time, this unlucky accident plagued Ericsson's career like a malevolent star; and yet, it was he who designed the "cheesebox on a raft" known as the *Monitor.*

In this, Ericsson incorporated all of the new designs and developments in shipbuilding which had followed upon the introduction of artillery ammunition. Up until the advent of explosive shell, solid shot striking a wooden ship often were no more effective than a handful of musket balls hurled at a

---

* A knot is a unit of speed equaling one nautical mile (6,080.20 feet) per hour. In naval parlance when a ship is "doing" say, 13 knots, she is traveling at 13 nautical miles per hour.

house. Frequently, spent shot bounced harmlessly on a ship's decks or off its hull, unless, of course, it happened to knock off some poor seaman's head; or else it lodged ineffectually in the hull or even plugged up holes made by predecessors. It was because of this that so many sea fights were fought at the murderous range of "half-pistol shot" or fifty feet. At such close quarters, as with *Bonhomme Richard* against *Serapis,* the bloodiest work was often done by sharpshooting marines stationed in a warship's "fighting tops." But when explosive shells appeared, the age of "wooden ships and iron men," of those romantic "wooden walls" which were Britain's first line of defense, was blown into obsolescence. Accordingly, ship-makers began to armor their vessels with iron plating.

Of course, there were ironclads long before *Monitor* and *Merrimac.* During the sixteenth century the Koreans beat back a Japanese invasion with "turtle ships" designed by Admiral Yi-Sun-Sin. These humped-back vessels were plated with iron and studded with spikes, and they may be considered the first of the ironclads. Moreover, most navies had adopted shell ammunition, and as early as 1854 the Anglo-French naval forces had shelled the Russian Black Sea port of Sevastopol during the Crimean War. Nevertheless, the clash at Hampton Roads was the first engagement between shell-firing ironclads. Furthermore, Ericsson gave gunnery a great shove forward when he equipped *Monitor* with a revolving turret firing a pair of 11-inch muzzle-loaders which were withdrawn inside the turret for reloading. It was the turret that was to be revolutionary, for guns mounted in turrets located either on the forward or after decks of a ship, or sometimes even on the waist or quarters alongside the superstructure, changed the contour of the battleship. Gone were the gunports cut in one or two rows from stem to stern on either side of the ships. With the next American innovation, the superimposition of one turret upon another, that is, a high turret above a low one, even more firepower was packed onto the decks of a fighting ship. Finally, although these turrets generally could traverse an arc of only 180 degrees, rather than make a full 360-degree turn like *Monitor*'s round turret, they enabled a warship to swivel *all* its guns to either side, thus doubling the firepower available to the broadside ship.

Simultaneous with the appearance of the turret, and again a product of the American Civil War, was the emergence of another new type of warship: the cruiser. This was the name given to swift, unarmored vessels carrying sixteen 10-inch or 11-inch guns. Such armament, of course, was usually reserved for a battleship; but the cruiser was to show its worth as a commerce-destroying or blockading vessel, and eventually would be of great service in bombarding enemy coasts.

Some nations also built "battle cruisers," warships mounting guns as heavy as 14-inch but unencumbered by a "battlewagon's" thick armor-plating. Battle cruisers were more a European than an American naval concept, especially among the Germans with their fixation on commerce-destroying. Eventually, cruisers came to be divided between "light" and "heavy" classifications, the first mounting guns of from 3 to 6 inches in caliber, the second from 8 to 12 inches. Essentially, however, the appearance of the submarine and the cruiser in the Civil War rounded out the complement of fighting gun-fire ships.

Curiously enough, though, the *Monitor-Merrimac* battle did not immediately demonstrate the supremacy of steel-clad, gun-firing steamships. On the contrary, both before and after the Civil War a wide variety of ships was designed by naval architects eager to create a new queenship of battle. Among them was the ram, nothing less than an ironclad, sophisticated throwback to the days of beaked galleys at Salamis. *Merrimac* was herself primarily a rammer, and the very inconclusiveness of her slugging match with *Monitor* seemed to suggest the superiority of armor over gunfire. In fact, the Federal Navy built many a ram after Hampton Roads, some of them being pointed at both ends and looking like nothing so much as huge, elongated clothing irons. When ramming tactics triumphed for the Austrians over the Italians during the Battle of Lissa in 1866, the ram appeared supreme on the sea.

However, the ram was anything but a versatile ship. It could transport nothing, could not put troops ashore, could not bombard, could not, in the end, even defend itself against gunfire ships equipped with the best armor-piercing ammunition. So the crown went to the battleship, and the first genuine modern battleship was probably Britain's *Devastation*, completed in 1873. She was modern because she was steam-propelled, built of iron, armored, had her guns mounted in turrets and was completely devoid of sails and rigging. Up until *Devastation*, most steamships were also rigged for sail; in fact, many a die-hard old sea dog looked upon the ship's engines as being "auxiliary." But the Battle of Lissa, while falsely seeming to prove the superiority of armor over artillery, had truly demonstrated the need for a clear field of fire for a ship's armament, and that meant heaving the obstructive masts and sails over the side. Oddly enough, even as *Devastation* appeared, built to the orthodox warship proportions of 5 to 1 in length and width ("beam"), the Russians produced a circular battleship called the *Novgorod* but actually known as the *"popoffka"* after her slightly unorthodox designer, Admiral Popoff. The *popoffka* was 101 feet in diameter, mounting a brace of 11-inchers sited side by side on a platform, and because she was intended for coastal defense she seems to have been nothing more than a floating battery. However, it was the orthodox elongated warship that ultimately triumphed, and as she shed her sails in the process, she became absolutely dependent on coal, and later on oil.

Because the steam-driven warship required fuel, naval bases were ever more necessary to the nation seeking sea power; and this, as much as any other factor, gave rise to the era of "navalism." Navalism also led to an armaments race which produced the last great change in ship design before the advent of the aircraft carrier. This was the all-big-gun or "dreadnought" class of battleship. Prior to its appearance, battleships carried a mixed armament of large and medium guns. Such mixtures were difficult to control because accurate spotting was all but impossible with so many differences in shell-size, rate of loading, flight time and fall of shot. To be effective, a mixed-armament ship needed to close to ranges as short as 3,000 yards. Obviously, the answer was a uniform armament of big guns which could fire accurately from as far away as 12,000 yards. Yet, because of the innate conservatism of admirals as well as generals, and every navy's understandable reluctance to build an all-big-gun battleship that would make all its other leviathans obsolete, the all-big-gun battleship had to await the proof of battle. This came when Japan annihilated a Russian fleet at the Battle of Tsushima in 1905. After it became clear that it had not been the Japanese torpedoes which accomplished this stunning overthrow, but rather the fire of the Japanese 12-inch guns, Britain went ahead with plans for an all-big-gun battleship. This, the famous *Dreadnought*, was launched in 1906 and was ready for trials a year later. When she appeared upon the ocean, she outmoded every other battleship afloat, and the pace of the navalism scramble became ever more frantic.

Ironically, these enormously expensive dreadnoughts experienced a relatively short reign at sea. They fought in massed formations only twice, the first encounter coming when Britain's Grand Fleet collided with Germany's High Seas Fleet during the Battle of Jutland in 1915. This contest, incidentally, is another example of one force suffering a strategic defeat while winning a tactical victory. Although the Germans carried the day by giving more than they got, they were nevertheless forced to seek a sanctuary from which they never again emerged—thus leaving their country exposed to the scourge of the British blockade.

The second and last time dreadnoughts fought in line of battle was in 1944 at the Battle of Leyte Gulf, when the guns of American battleships and cruisers put the last-but-one Japanese dreadnought beneath the waves of Surigao Strait. In this epoch-ending engagement, the line-ahead tactics of ships-of-the-line fighting introduced three full centuries earlier also sank into the sea. And for the last time in naval history was there a record of the devastating tactic of "crossing the T," the maneuver by which one fleet puts itself broadside to the other fleet approaching in line-ahead formation and thus is able to bring all its big guns to bear while the foe cannot. This was what happened when Admiral Jesse Oldendorf put his battle fleet horizontal to the advance of Admiral Shoji Nishimura's force.

Actually, battleship supremacy ended at Jutland, for the new queenship of the waves—the aircraft carrier—was already afloat. Here, the French were the pioneers, having in 1913 fitted the cruiser *Foudre* to carry two aircraft. However, aircraft carriers did not really appear until after World War I and the attempt by the Washington Treaty of 1920 to put an end to navalism. After this agreement limited the size of both navies and warships, the United States decided to convert two 40,000-ton battle cruisers of a type disallowed by the treaty into aircraft carriers. These were the mighty *Lexington* and *Saratoga*, which were not to be surpassed until World War II.

During that conflict, of course, the carrier ruled supreme. Time and again the "flattop" demonstrated that command of the sea is now held by the navy that commands the air above it. True enough, land-based air sometimes contributed to the naval air battles of that struggle, and land-based aircraft such as the German Focke-Wulf Condors striking at Murmansk-bound American supply convoys rounding the north coast of Norway were also very effective. Generally speaking, however, and including even today's long-range, land-based aviation, control of the waves still depends on command of the

skies, perhaps even, as submarines grow more and more effective, of the depths beneath them. However, the carrier and the
submarine were not the only vessels to be so highly developed
during World War II. The exigencies of that global struggle
afloat called forth a whole host of auxiliary ships, especially
among the Americans fighting history's first true two-ocean
war.

There were smaller versions of the destroyer known as
destroyer-escorts and small escort-carriers, both very effective
in antisubmarine warfare, as well as minesweepers, mine-
layers, gunboats, rocket ships and PT boats, all of which may
be regarded as warships; and among the noncombat or supporting vessels there was an even larger array of ammunition
ships, store ships, cargo ships, all manner of tenders, command ships, hospital ships, surveying ships, oilers, troop trans-
ports, net-laying ships, gasoline ships, barracks ships, a variety
of repair ships, salvage vessels, tugboats, rescue vessels, landing ships for infantry, tanks and vehicles, an enormous variety
of landing craft, weather patrol ships, floating docks, patrol
cutters, a host of "unclassified" vessels, and even, so great was
the ingenuity of seagoing Americans, distilling ships. For all
of these different classifications, however, a navy's fighting
ships remain limited to aircraft carrier, battleship, cruiser and
destroyer, in that order of size.

Even today in Vietnam the United States Navy operates
with much the same warships. Aircraft still fly from its carrier
decks. Destroyers and cruisers still give the carriers protecting
screens, and still operate as radar pickets or bombardment
ships. Even the battleship is still useful for bombardment
missions, as it was in Korea. Moreover, sea power has again
conquered the enormous logistics problem of supplying a
battlefront thousands of miles away. No other means of con-
veyance is quite so cheap or ample as a ship's bottom, especially when it is not menaced by enemy aircraft or submarines.
Nor is anything more direct. The high seas are open to every-

one. There is no problem of violating any nation's airspace. The coasts of the world are available to sea power, especially those shores of what is called "the rim lands," all those peninsular formations or outcroppings which contain the Communist Eurasian land mass from the Norwegian Sea to the Sea of Okhotsk, from Norway through Western Europe through Arabia, India and Southeast Asia to Korea.

It is still true, as Winston Churchill said: "Sea power is a wonderful thing, once it is understood."

11. HOW CALL IT TREASON

Because this book is being written at a time when the Vietnam War appears to have sundered the American nation into rival camps of "hawks" and "doves," it seems fitting to include a chapter on dissent in war.

In the first place, dissent is not, as some distraught Americans seem to believe, a departure from American tradition but rather a return to it. Therefore, when newspapers and TV news programs are filled with films of young men burning their draft cards, young women burning the national flag or priests pouring blood on Federal draft records, all to protest the alleged "immorality" or "illegality" of the war in Vietnam, the fact is that the American nation is not witnessing anything new in its history. Some of these activities do seem to exceed the bounds of honest dissent to become forms of "giving aid and comfort to the enemy," as the Constitution defines treason. Whether or not this is so is a moot point, and it would be difficult to make a judgment without knowing the minds and hearts of the dissenters. What can be said, however, is that dissent in war, so far from being some disturbing new manifestation of "disloyalty," is rather only the most extreme expression of democracy's age-old dilemma of how to reconcile liberty with authority. And it is a problem which seems to be more or less difficult in exact proportion to the degree in which the war is either limited or total.

When American wars were limited and the commonwealth itself did not seem to be in danger, the government was free to tolerate dissent. But when the war was total, when it was

161

felt that the life of the nation was at stake, or that some mighty effort was required demanding an absolute unity among the people, then dissent was either ruthlessly suppressed, as with Woodrow Wilson in World War I, or it was made unpopular by some unifying outburst of national passion such as the sense of outrage succeeding the Japanese attack on Pearl Harbor in World War II. Whether or not Franklin D. Roosevelt would have followed Wilson's lead of jailing or silencing all those who opposed America's entry into war is another moot point. It does not seem likely that he could have tolerated dissent of the type which Wilson suppressed. But to speculate on the subject is academic, if only because the Japanese blunder at Pearl Harbor solved the problem for him.

However, it was only in these two world wars—the total wars—that dissent was not heard. Unfortunately, these were the two conflicts that shaped the concept of warfare held by most adult Americans. That is why they were so shocked and alarmed by the behavior of dissenters who did not scruple to invade federal draft offices to seize and burn draft records. Yet, in all of the other American wars, the limited ones, there was always widespread criticism of and opposition to the war effort; sometimes to a degree of disloyalty, if not outright treachery, that would make the outcries of modern "doves" seem a comparatively subdued clucking indeed.

Dissent existed in the very beginning of our history, during the little backwash wars of the colonial period, when Frontenac's fortress at Quebec was often supplied by the enemy ports of New England. It persisted through the Revolution, when the Tories and neutralists together represented close to half the population. In 1780, when Washington's army numbered only 9,000 men, there were 8,000 Tories fighting for King George. There were also plenty of Tories present at the gala farewell party given for Lord Howe in Philadelphia, although beautiful Peggy Shippen, the love of the dashing young Captain André's life, was not permitted to attend because her father would not allow her to wear the Turkish bloomers required for female merrymakers. Lucky (or unlucky) for lovely Peggy, because when the British went out of Philadelphia and the Patriots came in, the Patriots blackballed all who attended the gala, leaving Peggy free to meet and marry a charming Continental general named Benedict Arnold.

As is well known, dissent was fierce during the War of 1812, derided as "Mr. Madison's war" and particularly hateful to New England, which found it so inimical to its own interests that it considered seceding from the Union. What is not generally known is that Sir George Prevost's splendid army in Canada was fed and supplied by New York and Vermont. Sir George's most difficult decision, as he prepared to invade the United States, was whether to move along the west (New York) or the east (Vermont) side of Lake Champlain. At last he decided: "Vermont has shown a disinclination to the war, and as it is sending in specie [as well as] provisions, I will confine offensive operations to the west side of Lake Champlain." Because New York had not been as ardent as Vermont in the enemy's cause, it was her soil that was to be ravaged.

Dissent as derisive and vituperative as the present criticism of the war in Vietnam also characterized the Mexican War. New England, once again, was the center of opposition. Daniel Webster suggested that President Polk should be impeached for provoking the war, and many ministers vowed that they would rather fight on the other side. Senator Thomas Corwin of Ohio came to be known as Black Tom for his remark: "If I were a Mexican, I would tell you: 'Have you not room in your own country to bury your dead men? If you come into mine, we will meet you with bloody hands, and welcome you to hospitable graves.' " Abraham Lincoln did not go quite so far, but his denunciation of Polk as a liar eventually cost him his seat as a Whig congressman.

As President, Lincoln brutally silenced dissent at the outset of the Civil War, only tolerating it after he had made sure of the allegiance of the border states. Thereafter, Lincoln had his troubles with Peace Democrats and Copperheads,* some of whom did not hestitate to excoriate him as a "gorilla tyrant." And if the radical Republicans who believed that Lincoln was not fighting the war hard enough could name a splinter candidate for President, the Copperheads who branded the war "a most bloody and costly failure" were strong enough to compel the Democratic party to accept a peace platform at its national convention. In the South, President Jefferson Davis also wore the hairshirt of opposition and dissent. The intransigence of such "states' rights" governors as Brown of Georgia and Vance of North Carolina helped to hamstring the Confederate war effort. Brown raised a militia of 10,000 men to defend his state alone, and Vance, only less obstructionist, had to contend with antiwar sentiment so strong that at one point there were open calls for North Carolina to secede from the Confederacy.

United again, America's next limited war was with Spain, and in this conflict the Anti-Imperialist League led by Americans such as Mark Twain, William James, Andrew Carnegie, labor leader Samuel Gompers, President Eliot of Harvard, President Jordan of Stanford and the poet William Vaughn Moody bitterly opposed the "annexation" of the Philippines as a crime against liberty.

When the Philippine Insurrection erupted under Emilio Aguinaldo, these same people deliberately urged young men not to volunteer or enlist in that "criminal enterprise." Carnegie appointed himself hairshirt to the Republican administration, bombarding its members with sarcastic or denunciatory letters. To Whitelaw Reid of the pro-Republican New York *Tribune* he wrote: "It is a matter of congratulation that you seem to have about finished your work of civilizing the

---

* Antiwar Northerners came to be known as "Copperheads" from the Indian heads they cut from copper pennies to wear in their lapels.

Filipinos. It is thought that about eight thousand of them have been completely civilized and sent to Heaven."

Scurrilous pamphlets denouncing the alleged duplicity of the McKinley government were mailed to troops in the Philippines; and the War Department, exercising no such restraint as has guided the Johnson and Nixon administrations in Vietnam, declared the literature seditious and seized it. Dissent in this instance not only led to the suppression of free speech at home, it also encouraged Aguinaldo to fight on; and he quoted endlessly from the antiwar pamphlets of a retired textile manufacturer named Edward Atkinson.

Enter the twentieth century, and with it the two world wars in which dissent was suppressed or made unpopular and from which many Americans derived their concept of war as "total." Enter next the Nuclear Age, in which total war could mean only total annihilation. Willy-nilly, America had to fight limited wars again, the first of which was in Korea. During the Korean War, dissent reappeared. It was not, however, the sort of popular protest which usually begins among clergymen, writers and educators before it spreads to the general public. The Korean dissent was almost exclusively political. Senator Taft's scornful description of the conflict as "Mr. Truman's War" was typical. To the general public, Korea was merely repugnant, not "outrageous" or "immoral," and this was probably because most Americans still thought of war in terms of complete "victory" or of the "all-out" effort which crushes the enemy and leaves him prostrate. The concept of a limited war such as the one in Korea was alien to them.

Unfortunately, to such a habit of mind, the concept of dissent in war is equally distasteful, and this accounts for much of the anger which many Americans feel when they see dissenters flout the nation's laws with impunity. Certainly, some of the protesters are not lovable, especially when they declare openly that withdrawal from Vietnam is worth any price, including the denial of free speech to representatives of our government. Nor is there a shred of doubt that their dissent has encouraged the enemy. Ho Chi Minh has said again and again that the dissenter represents the true American attitude. This may put him in the company of all of America's other limited-war enemies—King George III, Lord Liverpool, Santa Anna, Aguinaldo, Kim Il Sung and Mao Tse-tung—but it is nonetheless a fact which must be faced. How much dissent hurts the war efforts has to be balanced against how much may be lost by encroaching upon the First Amendment, a policy which very likely would make America the less worth fighting for.

In essence, then, the problem is a balancing act: liberty in one scale, authority in the other. The problem is what Abraham Lincoln thought might be the "inherent and fatal weakness" of free government, when he asked: "Must a government, of necessity, be too strong for the liberties of its own people, or too weak to maintain its own existence?" In itself, dissent is probably a good thing, perhaps especially in war. Hitler's great mistake was in attacking Russia while Britain remained unconquered, with the United States obviously preparing to come to her side. Errors of such magnitude are simply not possible in a society which permits criticism to exist. It is also certain that the mood of black hatred which gripped the Allied peoples in World War I was chiefly responsible for the Carthaginian peace which led to World War II. Voices critical of the Treaty of Versailles simply were not heeded. Hatred also stilled any voice that might have been raised against President Roosevelt's calamitous policy of Unconditional Surrender for the Axis powers.

Criticism of the struggle in Vietnam, therefore, has been a healthy condition which has probably compelled Johnson and Nixon and their advisers to consider public reaction to every decision to "escalate" the war. It also must have had much to do with their anxiety to bring the Communists to the conference table.

Nevertheless, the First Amendment cannot be rewritten as the Magna Carta of the Sovereign Citizen. No one in a democracy is free to pick and choose his obligations. All citizens are obliged to obey decisions of the general citizenry, even when they disagree. If a man's disagreement springs from his conscience, then he has the duty to speak out against the decision. He has not, however, the right to interfere with others who wish to implement that decision. One cannot make a dictator out of one's own conscience. Thoreau went to jail for refusing to pay a poll tax for the Mexican War, but he did not attempt to prevent other Americans from paying theirs. It is true that at times civil disobedience may become a duty, but it can never be a right. Any government so recognizing it would not long endure, for when freedom becomes perfect among imperfect human beings, society has come full cycle to that state called anarchy.

Some dissenters reply that when their verbal protests are ignored (meaning that the government has not done what they told it to do), they have the right to take "direct action." To compel American withdrawal from this "immoral war," they have the right to destroy property, private as well as public, to obstruct the war effort and to disturb the peace generally. This is the credo of the Sovereign Citizen, who calls his violence the "new form" of dissent. But no less a revolutionary than Rousseau wrote: "As soon as it is possible to disobey with impunity, disobedience is legitimate; and, the strongest being always in the right, the only thing that matters is to act so as to become the strongest."

It is difficult to ignore the faith in force underlying the activities of many of today's dissenters, the people I have been calling Sovereign Citizens. They seem to believe that minorities have higher rights than majorities. They do not seem to be interested in education but only in agitation, in heat rather than light. Certainly, they do not seem to understand or care about the limits of free speech. Free speech is not free shouting by which one man can drown out the voices of those who disagree with him. Protest is not defiance, because a government defied is a government weakened. Nor is the freedom to assemble or to demonstrate the freedom to destroy or abuse or to interfere with someone else's legitimate freedom.

Finally, if any democratic society is to survive, dissent must be loyal. It is one thing for a dissenter to cry, "Down with Johnson!" but quite another to shout, "Hurray for Ho!" Although the right to dissent is surely guaranteed by the First Amendment it does not include the right to cheer for the enemy.

12. WHAT IS A WAR?

If there has been one characteristic manifested by both the "hawks" and the "doves" of the Vietnam War, it has been their ignorance of the nature of war. With only a few exceptions, they simply did not and do not know what war is all about. To explain war, of course, is the purpose of this book; and so, these last three chapters will be devoted to a discussion of the institution itself.

To begin: what is war? The answer is that war is socially sanctioned armed conflict between hostile groups.

The operative word here is "hostile." During war, battle or combat may alternate with periods of noncombat, but the fact of hostility is always constant. It is this that distinguishes war from an armed intervention, such as in Lebanon, where there was no fighting; from reprisals, such as the recurrent border raids between Israel and the Arab states; from armed neutralities such as the American attitude toward the Axis in the early part of World War II; from piracy and banditry, or from mob violence such as the riots which have tormented our cities during the past few years. It is the cessation of hostilities that brings a war to an end; either by an armistice followed by a treaty, as in World War I; by an armistice and the failure to arrange a treaty, as in Korea; or simply by a fading away of hostilities, as in Greece and Turkey in 1947–48 when the Communist guerrillas simply dropped their guns and stopped fighting. Because human beings are so legalistic in these matters, and because a definite ending date is always sought so as to clarify

169

veterans' rights, combat pay and other considerations, a fade-away war may be ended by Proclamation, as Teddy Roosevelt proclaimed the Philippine Insurrection at an end on the Fourth of July, 1902.

War, then, is socially sanctioned armed conflict between hostile groups, or even groups of groups, as between military alliances; and it is not, as some writers have suggested, an activity comparable to a fist fight between individuals, or even to a duel. One of mankind's immemorial mistakes, and also frequently a cause of war, is to consider nations to be collections of individuals acting in concert just as the individual man acts alone. The truth, however, is that nations are far more sensitive to such concepts as "honor" or "prestige" than individuals are.

It is a rare man indeed who will risk all that he loves and owns in a contest with some insulting or trespassing neighbor. But nations do this constantly, and often with an enthusiasm rivaled only by the remorse which follows; for the war dance always ends in a dirge. Why this is so is for social scientists to answer; although it may well be that individual men, having surrendered all forms of violent coercion to the nation in exchange for security, thereupon invest the nation with a sacredness which they do not assign to their own flesh and furniture. Perhaps this springs from a man's habit of looking for some transcendent cause with which to ennoble his own dreary, day-to-day existence. This willingness to sacrifice, even to die, for something better than themselves is one of the finest qualities in men; unfortunately, these shining ideals and poetic symbols often become the mask for the terrible demons which dwell within them. Calling themselves ready to die for a cause, they are actually more prepared to kill for it. Whatever the explanation of this attitude, the fact remains that there is nothing more sensitive on earth than a nation-state.

This is the big boggle which thwarts every attempt to

form a world organization charged with keeping the peace. Always, the question is raised: how do you punish a sovereign state? The answer is that, so far, no way has been found; and until one is, wars will continue. Even the medieval kings thought of themselves as being responsible to a Supreme Being, but nation-states hold themselves responsible to themselves alone. They acknowledge no higher authority, at least not in the sensitive areas of national honor or integrity.

This is the basic problem in international affairs, the solution of which would do much to end the tensions and conflicts which produce war. It is not likely, however, that nation-states will *ever* surrender their sovereignty. If any solution is forthcoming, it probably will be given by *men*, not nations. Once men get over the dangerous habit of taking some ideal, some concept, some name—be it "the church" or "my country" or "our crowd"—and charging it with that furious, demonic drive which they rarely assign to themselves personally, it would seem that they would be on their way to a true international community. Men who have moved from the sovereignty of the individual (which is to say, anarchy) into the sovereignty of clan, tribe, kingdom and nation-state, would then stop thinking of themselves as Americans, Arabs and Chinese, as Europeans, Africans and Asians, and begin to think of themselves as Worldlings. To do this is not to surrender sovereignty but to shift it to a higher level. International law, superseding national law, would then reach into every city and hamlet; and men would hold themselves no longer accountable to a nation but to the generally accepted codes of mankind. As Teilhard de Chardin said: "The age of nations is past. The task before us now, if we would not perish, is to build the earth." This, of course, is a very large order, one which will take a little time to fill. But it seems to be the answer, and it is to be hoped that men are not delayed along the way by some intermediate or regional stage; that is, a world trifurcated among Africans, Asians and Europeans, for then we shall have "1984," which is to say a state of "wardom," and probably World War III. After that, as Albert Einstein said: "The next World War will be fought with stones."

Let us, however, propose that a truly international order would be capable of establishing peace. What, then, is peace? Is it birdsong in a field of flowers beside a babbling brook? Hardly. Is it definable at all? Again, hardly. Many a peace movement has foundered on the rock of finding a suitable definition for peace. Some philosophers argue that peace is not an intelligible concept without a world order. Pacifists insist that peace can be defined only negatively; that peace is the absence of war. Their reasoning here is subtle. They say that if peace is given a positive definition, it will then become one of those demonic symbols of which I have been speaking, and people will go to war to establish peace! In a way, they are right; for there has been many a war fought to end war or to keep the peace. William Tecumseh Sherman said, "The object of war must be a better peace," and in this sagacious observation he seems to uphold the fears of the pacifists. However, when pacifists hold that no form of violence can be justified—not even to obtain peace—they are flying once again in the face of reality. They are inviting the attack of the aggressor.

Perhaps, if war is described as a period of hostility, peace may be defined as a period of cooperation. Men and groups cooperate because they can perceive the advantage to be gained in granting others the same privileges and rights which they seek for themselves. Peace, then, is the notion of the common good. Unfortunately, the rub here is that nations sometimes believe they are serving the common good by going to war; and because the most successful form of cooperation, either voluntary or imposed, is usually a characteristic of a nation at war, the definition seems to be inadequate.

What about St. Augustine's definition of peace as "tranquillity in order"? First it must be assumed that the order is a just one. But even then tranquillity does not always prevail. Domestic peace is constantly broken by criminals and wrongdoers, world peace by hostile nations in armed conflict. Even a world society charged with keeping peace would have to use force, against either individual men or groups of men, and that would not be a peaceful condition. Has any man ever known a moment of real peace or tranquillity? Are men not always in the grip of some conflict or tension? This is what St. James, meant, I think, when he wrote: "Whence are wars and contentions among ye; are they not hence, from your lusts, which war in your members?"

Apparently, all the world is in conflict: the wind against the wave, nature "red in tooth and claw," men against nature, against other men and against themselves. The very word conflict seems to describe history. As Robert Louis Stevenson wrote:

> The drums of war, the drums of peace,
> Roll through our cities without cease,
> And all the iron halls of life
> Ring with the unremitting strife.

Not as lovely or as incisive, but just as perceptive, Karl von Clausewitz, that much-quoted, seldom-read and little-understood theorist of war, remarks: "We say therefore War belongs to the province of social life. It is a conflict of great interests which is settled by bloodshed, and only in that is it different from others."*

Conflict again: it is always and everywhere. Peace, pacifism, so-called tranquillity simply do not exist. When men are completely passive, they are dead. How aptly did Jeremiah cry: "Peace, peace—and there was no peace." There never

---

* All quotations from Clausewitz are from his *On War*, 3 vols. (New York: Barnes & Noble, 1966).

was, never has been, and probably never will be that illusive, indefinable constancy which we call "peace."

Why am I so vehement, so extreme? Because I wish an end to self-delusion, to starry-eyed beguilement with the candy-coated myth of "a world without war." It is simply not possible, not as long as man remains the instinctively aggressive animal that he is, constantly in conflict with himself and those around him. One might as well talk of a world without crime, and thus ignore man as acquisitive and selfish. It is a grave error to think of man as a pacific creature. Pacifism is not an instinct, like aggression. It is an ideal, like charity. Pacifism is not even the opposite of aggression, for who is more aggressive than a pacifist? No, like charity which man needs to cultivate in order to limit and control his basic selfishness, pacifism is a noble state to which he can only aspire. He can never hope to make it permanent, however. And yet, by constantly aspiring to it, he might possibly make *war* less permanent.

13. OF WAR AND PEACE

One of Karl von Clausewitz's favorite themes was that war is a part of man's social activity. Until recently, it has proved most efficacious for mankind. It made civilization. Primitive warfare, by encouraging group solidarity, by cultivating the virtues of courage, loyalty and obedience, made social creatures of men. By the very fact of his organization for war, social man conquered antisocial man and enrolled him in society. Walter Bagehot, has said: "Civilization begins, because the beginning of civilization is a military advantage." And: "The compact tribes win."

Political structure, the division of labor, tools, the use of metals and machinery, all of these were born of war, not of peace; and it is from the powder horn of Mars, not the cornucopia of some unknown goddess of tranquillity, that most of mankind's inventions and innovations have poured. Only as war has begun to brutalize us, to diminish our capacity for compassion, to become increasingly destructive, has it commenced to offset its earlier advantages; so that now, war, having made civilization, threatens to destroy what it has made. Because of this, because of our fear of nuclear holocaust, we are all constrained to control or limit it, or even, among some very hopeful men, to eliminate it.

Scientists of the social disciplines say that war is an outmoded function, like the water wings with which a child learns to swim, and that the pugnacious instinct upon which it feeds can be controlled by education, law and ethics. Behavioral biologists suggest that man's aggressive drives

175

can be diverted or "ritualized" into harmless forms. Econo-mists of the Norman Angell school maintain that once men realize that "war does not pay" they will consign it to the dustbin of history, along with human sacrifice, slavery, witchburning and the torture of witnesses. Jurists and political leaders, of course, look to a world society for salvation; while people of no particular discipline such as myself wonder if mankind's deep-seated need for opposition of some sort, the habit of searching for devils to be "agin," cannot be supplied by the distraction of exploring space.

One reason social scientists say war is a social function and not instinctive is their discovery of primitive tribes who do not wage war. (Napoleon, incidentally, became outraged when he heard that the Okinawans neither made nor carried arms.) However, these unwarlike tribes (who do commit multiple murders) are also the most backward and isolated; and once they come into contact with advanced and warlike people, they adopt the practice and progress. In other words, they have the capacity for war, which is only to say the power to organize their pugnacious instincts. So the behavioral biologists seem to be correct in seeing war as the result of men's inherent aggressiveness.

Konrad Lorenz, one of the most perceptive, insists that aggression is indispensable to the survival of mankind. Few animals can survive without the instinct, he declares, and goes so far as to say: "It is a fact worthy of deep meditation that for all we know the bond of personal friendship was evolved by the necessity for certain individuals to cease from fighting each other in order more effectively to combat other fellow-members of the species." From friendship and clan it is only a short evolutionary step to kingdoms and nations; so here again aggression emerges as a definite value. But if Lorenz is convinced that aggression is not only necessary and innate, but also ineradicable, he acknowledges that now, under the dreadful Sign of the Mushroom Cloud, men must do something about controlling it.

His prescription is that men, like many of the animals he has observed, learn to divert or "ritualize" that fondness for fighting which threatens to destroy our species. He suggests that international sport is probably the best means of doing this. Rugged sports such as mountain-climbing or ocean sailing, while supplying the element of danger characteristic of war, also cultivate the valuable warrior virtues of courage, loyalty and obedience while encouraging the spirit of self-sacrifice. Sporting contests between nations would not only provide an outlet for what he calls the "militant enthusiasm" of nations, but also promote friendship between peoples of different nations.

With all due respect to Lorenz, it is difficult to overlook all those international soccer matches which have ended in riots and sometimes death. The Greeks, who invented the Olympics, were also fairly warlike; and it is a rare modern Olympiad that does not produce an international squabble or two.

This is not to say that sport can be a cause of war, but it is to suggest that it can promote the ill will which leads to it. Sport is too much like war. It is a contest which also ends in victory or defeat, in which "something is at stake," and in which "national honor" can become involved. (One wonders if a national sense of humor might not serve as a splendid escape valve for that supersensitive national sense of honor.)

Actually, it does not seem likely that God, nature or evolution, whichever force it was that commanded the blind obedience of animals in controlling the aggression that threatened to destroy them, can do the same with rational-irrational, self-willed men. *We* can choose. When we cease to have the power of choice, we will cease to be men. Therefore, one is inclined to agree with William James: "Our ancestors have bred pugnacity into our bone and marrow, and thousands of years of peace won't breed it out of us." The best that can be hoped from the study of our instincts is the destruction of that pernicious myth of man "the peace-loving animal," of that boomeranging bromide that "men are basically good." When Robert Frost heard the title of Carl Sandburg's poem, *"The People, Yes,"* he shook his head gently, murmuring: "And the People, No." The people, yes; and the people, no—here is a poetic definition of what Christianity calls Original Sin, an unpopular doctrine which even the great evangelizer of evolution, Thomas Huxley, maintained was nevertheless a sincere attempt to explain the obviously wounded nature of mankind.

But let us say that there is no Original Sin, with its concomitant of free choice. Let us say that science can devise a "peace pill" which will make everyone peaceful, all of us disposed to choose only the good. Who will be the first to give it or receive it? Will the Arabs swallow it before the Israelis, the Communists before the Capitalists? Suppose we were all at once constrained to swallow the peace pill, we were all rid of our aggression. What, then, would become of the race? Probably, we would become the food of all those animals we are urged not to eat.

Aggression, moreover, is not the reigning instinct. Fear or the instinct for self-preservation also operates. When a boy confronts a man, it is likely that his instinct for aggression, though present, will retreat before the more powerful instinct of self-preservation, and the boy will defer to the man. The same may be said of a soldier. His aggression, his desire to impose his will on someone else, will always submit to a superior similar desire on the part of his opponent. Any student of war knows that battles are won, not by killing men, but by making them run. More men are killed in the pursuit than in the attack, from behind than in front. Finally, "aggression" will never survive the crash of the first artillery shell. Aggression, the willingness to fight, will get a man into uniform, into a foxhole even, but it is discipline that will keep him there. Soldierly discipline, an acquired characteristic, seems to be of much more military value than the instinct of aggression. Man's aggressive nature may explain why he fights, why he desires to impose his will upon others, but it will not explain war. And in modern times at least, the decision for war usually is made some time before the propaganda machinery for manipulating the citizenry's pugnacious instincts is set in motion.

War, then, is not explicable in biological terms. It seems to be rather a social, political and legal problem. War, as has been suggested, is socially approved armed conflict between hostile groups. If "hostility" is the condition of war, "groups" are its cause. What a man may gain from the structure and order of a group, he will also lose in frustration and conflict. Man is not only up against himself but society as well. Hermits do not commit murders, neither do they go to war. But social men do both. Once men come together, their individual interests collide; and when they organize into groups, the group interests are in conflict. When this occurs, and diplomatic efforts to resolve the conflict fails, what we call war ensues. Society itself seems to be the root cause of war, and as long as great societies—sovereign nation-states— continue to possess great and unchecked power, war will remain inevitable.

Some anthropologists might challenge that last statement. To them, the aggression that makes war possible is not an instinct at all but an acquired characteristic. Men were not formed pugnacious and hostile, they say, but only got that way. The fault, according to them, lies in the training of children. Parents who frustrate the impulses of their children by denying them, say, a second dish of ice cream in the interests of teaching them self-control, and who then punish them if they scream in resentment, are actually driving the child's aggressions underground, from whence they eventually emerge more horrible and destructive. If parents were more permissive, they contend, if children were not so frequently denied their desires, nor punished too severely when they resent those frustrations which are inescapable, they would not grow up to be such aggressive adults. Perhaps. But even the exponents of permissiveness will admit that they have no body of evidence to support their thesis. So profound a student of the human psyche as Sigmund Freud finally came to total rejection of the frustration-aggression theory. Freud decided ". . . that men are not gentle, friendly creatures wishing for love, who simply defend themselves if they are attacked, but that a powerful measure of desire for aggression has to be reckoned as part of their instinctual endowment."

My own limited experience with the children of permissive parents has convinced me that most of them are an unlovely compound of selfishness and cowardice, to say nothing of their bad manners. Meeting them, one has no desire to meet their parents. When they, too, reach maturity, the only consideration which curbs their aggression is that healthy fear of force which society at last instills in them.

It is force and force alone which restrains aggression. Peace is kept by the sword or the fear of the sword. A man who sees a sign saying "No Left Turn" will not turn left, simply because he fears the law backed up by force; and it is this same elementary fear which, carried up to the international level, may have a restrictive or limiting influence on the aggression of nations or international ideologies such as Communism. But to hope that a new type of emotional training will alter human nature seems far too hopeful.

Yet, if human nature will not change, Sir Norman Angell counters, it is still possible to change human behavior. True. Slavery and human sacrifice do seem to be headed for the ash can of history. Most men no longer believe that torture is either a moral or an efficient means of obtaining information. But men changed their attitudes to these customs when it was seen that they were *intrinsically* evil. If economists can prove that "war does not pay," as I think they have, they will have removed only the economic motive for war. But there are many others: to the drive for possession may be added those of power, pleasure, prestige and even principle. More important, to demonstrate the obvious waste of modern war only demonstrates its inefficiency, not its immorality.

This is because war is not basically immoral, like slavery or human sacrifice. War is only violence in its most organized extreme, and violence can be used or abused. There is certainly no defense for the violence by which a human sacrifice is deprived of his life or an innocent human being of his liberty; but there is much to be said for the violence by which a man resists an intruder, by which a policeman deprives a criminal of his freedom, by which free men shake off a tyrant's yoke or defend their country against aggression. War, then, can be moral or immoral, depending upon the intent of the combatants (a matter which I will discuss later); and it is time for us to stop applauding Benjamin Franklin for his silly remark, "There never was a good war or a bad peace." The War of the Revolution which he observed from Paris seems to have been a just one, and the peace which Communism seeks to impose on our world—a tranquillity ordered to slavery—seems very bad indeed.

Even the jurists and political leaders who work for a world order are agreed that war, per se, is not evil; and they expect their world society to employ force against any government or group which unjustly disturbs the peace of the world. Finally, those who hope that war might be eliminated by the distraction of space exploration are compelled to admit that this is, at best, a diversion; that if space can be colonized, the colonies can be fought for; that if we encounter other civilizations in space, it is not unlikely that we will fight them. (Let us hope that we do not lose; that we do not encounter superior corporeal beings; for then we will be surely eaten or enslaved.)

From all of these standpoints, then, it appears that war will not be eliminated, although it might be controlled or limited; and from the viewpoint of politics, of the appeal to arms as the last resort of the downtrodden, it may be desirable. Yet, there is one last position to be examined: the all-important ethical one.

What do the great religious teachers and the theologians say about war? In the East, there is the doctrine of ahimsa or nonviolence which characterizes some forms of Hinduism while permeating Buddhism and Jainism. In the belief that all creatures have souls as much as humans, life must everywhere be respected. "So pious Jains today will feed ants as a religious act, place cloths over their noses to prevent insects being drawn up their nostrils, and eat only by day to avoid accidents to insect life in the dark. The best death a Jain can die is by self-starvation."* Such a doctrine naturally abhors wars as the most extreme form of violence, and the fact that it is so widely held does much to explain why India has so often quivered beneath the boot of the conqueror.

Buddha also taught nonviolence, and it is worth noting that Buddhism's very pacifism was used by the Ming dynasty of China to curb the fierce Mongols. In 1570, a Ming statesman who knew Mongolia well declared: "Buddhism forbids bloodshed . . . ; for this reason we should do our utmost to diffuse that faith among the nomads." They did this with such success that Michael Prawdin remarks: "This is probably a unique instance of the use of religion as a means for rendering pacific a too powerful neighbor, of undermining the warlike spirit of a people by introducing a pacifist cult with an imposing ritual and much display, and with saints, demons and devils to capture their imagination. It is a unique instance, too, of checking the increase of a warlike population by inducing most of the potential warriors to become celibate monks. So successful was this policy, that, 'during the last fifty years of the Ming Dynasty there was no need to light a watch-fire on the boundaries of China.' "

---

* Percival Spear, *India,* The University of Michigan History of the Modern World (Ann Arbor: University of Michigan Press, 1961), p. 61.

If it is argued, "Well, at least nonviolence kept the Mongols from killing other people, from making war," the answer is that this is true—but only from the Ming standpoint. But let us imagine the chagrin and astonishment of Genghis Khan if he, like European travelers of the day, were to witness how a cult of nonviolence had transformed the descendants of his dreaded riders from "terrible, indefatigable, and cruel warriors into slothful, cowardly and docile camel-drivers and shepherds."

Yet, if the absolute pacifism of Buddhism is not to be recommended, neither is the absolute militance of Mohammedanism. Like the Iroquois of Northeastern America, Islam wore itself out on the warpath. Mohammedanism says simply that war to extend the domain of Islam is holy and that to die in a jehad or holy war against the infidel is to be transported to paradise.

In the faith of the Biblical Jews, the source of not only much of Islamic teaching but of Christianity as well, there existed a militance almost equally fierce. True, the Mosaic law does say, "Thou shalt not kill," but this seems to apply only to private murder; for Moses, who is also the author of the Jewish rules of war, says elsewhere: "But if [thy enemy] will not make peace, and shall begin war against thee, thou shalt besiege [their city]. And when the Lord thy God shall deliver it into thy hands, thou shalt slay all that are therein of the male sex with the edge of the sword." Actually, ancient Israel spoke constantly of Yahweh as "the God of Battles," and the bloodthirsty boasting of some prophets such as Samuel can become rather unpleasant reading. Nowhere in the Old Testament is there a denunciation of war as intrinsically evil.

What, then, of Christ? He spoke only twice of war. Once, He said: "What king, about to go to make war against another king, doth not first sit down and think whether he be able, with ten thousand, to meet him that with twenty thousand cometh against him?" In this, Jesus seems to be taking war for granted; and his parable is bound up with the simply military wisdom of avoiding battle with a superior foe. Another time he said: "And you shall hear of wars, and rumors of war." Here Jesus was only instructing his disciples in the events to occur before "the consummation of the world." However, He did not say, as a bellicose Marine general once furiously insisted in my presence: "There will *always* be war, and rumors of war." True, He did say, "Blessed are the peace-makers," to which only a madman would not say, "Amen"; and to Peter the impetuous He said, "All that take the sword shall perish by the sword," which could be either a stricture against violence or a condemnation of militarism. But He also said: "Do not think that I came to send peace upon earth: I came not to send peace, but the sword." By this, of course, He meant only that He was Truth itself, and that truth is always divisive. Nowhere, however, does the Prince of Peace denounce or decry war.

Whence, then, did Christian pacifism arise? Probably from the Sermon on the Mount, in which Christ blessed the poor in spirit, the meek, the merciful and the peacemakers. Early Christianity placed a pacifist interpretation on the Sermon, and so distinguished a saint and churchman as Martin of Tours won a discharge from the Roman Army because of his refusal to kill. One of my favorite saints is Maximilian, a Roman youth of about twenty-one, the son of a soldier, who refused to serve in the army with the statement: "I cannot enlist for I am a Christian." For this admirable, though I think misguided stand, Maximilian lost his head.

I say "misguided" because the Sermon on the Mount is for individuals and not for nations, and most especially has nothing to do with foreign policy. If, after Christianity became the official religion of the Roman Empire, the Christians had persisted in their pacifism, that would have meant the end of civilization. Rome after 313 (the year Constantine accepted Christianity) was pressed in on every side by pagan barbarians. Rome needed soldiers. Fortunately, a century later, Rome was rescued by the great St. Augustine, who understood a state's practical need for war.

Echoing Greeks such as Plato and Aristotle, who also had to meet the problem of individual as distinct from national ethics, Augustine originated the Christian doctrine of the "just war." A war was just if it was the only means of rectifying or preventing injustice, if no peaceful means were adequate or available, if the costs of war would not outweigh the injustice to be corrected, and if the proper authority, having considered all these conditions, gave its sanction to the war. In doubtful cases, the individual, bound to protect the society that protects him, must subordinate his judgment to that of the proper political authority. However, if the individual *knows* that his government is motivated by unjust rather than just intentions, he not only can but should refuse. In other words, if you trust your government, you must serve; if you don't, you should refuse. The difficulty, of course, is for an ordinary man to possess enough of the pertinent facts to make any such judgment.

During this century, however, and especially in our own time, a kind of idealistic or at least non-realistic thinking on war has informed the Christian position. Protestant sects such as the Quakers, of course, make pacifism an article of faith. War is absolutely unjust and immoral. With some pacifists who are not necessarily Christian, no individual has the right to take another person's life, not even in self-defense or in defense of another innocent person. This is the extreme attitude which, as this study has already suggested, has probably caused as many wars as aggression.

Official Catholic thinking has also changed, shifting to a vague idealism—born of the modern horror of war—which permits only a "defensive war," whatever that is. Foreign policy and national sovereignty being the intricate and sensitive things that they are, it is far from uncommon to find both

sides in a conflict claiming that they are defending themselves against aggression. To condone only "defensive war,"
as modern Catholicism and most Protestant sects now do, is
merely to sidestep the central issue of the morality of war
itself. Thus, the just war doctrine actually remains unchallenged, except among those doctrinal pacifists who denounce
but do not demonstrate the immorality of war.

What we call a war then is only unjust or immoral according to the intentions of the persons who cause it, and it is
entirely possible, as it is in all other conflict situations, that
the leaders of both sides may be sincerely convinced of the
justness of their cause. For the ordinary citizen to be able to
make this judgment, again, just does not seem possible. To
allow the individual to pick and choose his wars according
to their so-called "morality" is only to permit the Sovereign
Citizen to lead us back into anarchy. His government may
be mistaken, and he may be being asked to pay for the mistake with his life, but so also does he pay with his standard
of living or his life for government mistakes in the area of
economics or flood control. In its essence, then, war is no
more immoral or unjust than any other form of violence.
Only in its use or abuse may it be judged. Therefore, a moral
horror of war is not an acceptable plea for a refusal to serve
in one. Our government is not bound to accept it; it does so
only out of compassion and respect for religion. But to defer
conscientious objectors rather than to assign them to noncombat duty such as the medical corps seems a bit too compassionate. All who served in World War II admired the
courage of the movie star, Lew Ayres, because, though he
professed a horror of war, he nevertheless volunteered to drive
a front-line ambulance. But it was the rifleman, not the
ambulance driver, who stopped Hitler.

14. THE END OF IT ALL

If society itself is the cause of war, if the aggressive instinct makes war possible, what, then, are the reasons for war? From Antoine Henri Jomini comes a list of six reasons for international war. These are:

1. To reclaim certain rights or to defend them.

2. To protect and maintain the great interests of the state (as commerce, manufactures or agriculture).

3. To maintain the balance of power.

4. To propagate political or religious theories, to crush them, or to defend them.

5. To increase the influence and power of the state by acquisitions of territory.

6. To gratify a mania for conquest (or glory).

From this fairly comprehensive sextet let us take the first one: to reclaim or defend a right. Here is a simple explanation of the reason for our own Revolutionary War. Our colonial ancestors believed that the right to impose taxes was theirs alone, not Parliament's, and to defend this right they went to war. Here it seems to have been a truly "just war." From the fifth reason, however, the desire to acquire territory, spring examples of unjust war: our own expansionist war against Mexico or Frederick the Great's seizure of the Austrian province of Silesia in 1740, which triggered the War of the Austrian Succession. Frederick of Prussia had sworn to defend his beautiful young neighbor, Queen Maria Theresa of Austria; instead he chose to rob her and to increase his power at her expense.

But when Frederick did this he frightened his other European neighbors into a war for "the balance of power." This famous phrase means nothing more than the struggle among nations to see to it that no one among them becomes too strong for them all. As a result, nations are constantly shifting alliances so that today's foe is tomorrow's friend.

During World War II we fought the Germans and the Italians, but now the West Germans and the Italians are our allies in NATO, a military alliance erected to prevent our former ally, Soviet Russia, from becoming too strong in Europe. Japan was also our enemy in that conflict, but today she is our ally in the Cold War confrontation with Communist China. Actually, it would be much better for America if our government would openly admit that the Cold War is essentially a balance-of-power struggle. True enough, it has very strong ideological overtones; true also, Communism, or what I prefer to call the closed society, is the sworn enemy of our own open society. Yet, just because holy wars are the bloodiest and most destructive of all, and because people motivated by hatred of an enemy represented to be the incarnation of evil are prone to think of victory in terms of annihilation, it would be wiser to have Americans understand the very great possibility that, in the Far East at least, Russia and America may combine to restrain China. In other words, it is safer to think of war as an instrument of political policy rather than as the Almighty's avenging sword wielded by his Chosen People.

The basic difficulty of the balance-of-power principle is that each nation believes that it is good only for other nations, not for itself. Each nation strives to "hold" the balance of power, and thus eventually to establish a hegemony over all the others. When this happens, there is a war for empire; as in the Napoleonic Wars and the two world wars. To strive to "hold" the balance of power does not, however, automatically produce war. During the century between the defeat of

Napoleon and World War I, Britain "held" the balance of power. Because she was the world's foremost naval and commercial power, whichever side she took automatically became the stronger. Fortunately, she did not, by devouring first her enemies and then turning to consume her allies, give herself an attack of imperial indigestion. Instead, she used this unique power to "localize" the wars of Europe, to keep them from becoming general. She might have seized one-quarter of the earth's surface for her own, while ruling the world's preponderant element of water, as she did; but she did bestow the *Pax Britannica* on mankind; she did use her great strength more to encourage peace than to promote war.

That very *Pax Britannica*, incidentally, was broken when Kaiser Wilhelm sought to shift the balance of power in his own favor. And here is a war which seems to contain in itself almost every "reason" ever cited for the breakdown of peace; a conflict which makes it plain that General Jomini's six reasons, just because they are offered only from the politico-military standpoint, are actually inadequate. Other reasons for World War I, it has been argued, are the harshness of the Austrian ultimatum to Serbia after the assassination of the Austrian archduke; the assassination itself; the mobilization of Germany and Russia; the ambitions of the Kaiser; the growing naval and industrial rivalry between Germany and Britain; France's desire to recover Alsace-Lorraine or Austria's thrust to dominate the Balkans; the rise of militarism; the polarization of alliances into two huge armed camps; the greed of the munitions-makers; the stupidity of the diplomats; colonial rivalries, commercial rivalries, armament rivalries; the spirit of nationalism; the failure of humanism or of religion; the concept of sovereignty; the tendency of nations to expand; the inequalities of population distribution; the misguided faith in war as an instrument of policy; and many, many others. The list would be multiplied again if one were to study the character of Gavrilo Princip, the consumptive young madman who killed Archduke Ferdinand and his wife, to discover his hopes and fears, his sorrows and joys—in fact, the very emotional training of his childhood, on which the permissivists set such store, as well as the complete bundle of concepts and complexes, myths and delusions, theories and constructs which would have passed for the education of a young Serbian in the early part of the twentieth century.

Thus, to know the "reasons" for any war is to know almost everything about everyone involved in it. The reason for any kind of war is the reason for any kind of conflict of interests, and this is only to say again that war and peace are not mutually exclusive activities, as so many Americans seem to believe. They are both a part of man's social activity, and they both participate in each other. Even Clausewitz is imperfect when he says they differ only in the fact of bloodshed, because there is much blood shed during so-called peace. It is true, as he says, that the element of war is danger; yet there is also danger in peace. In my own opinion, hostility makes the difference, the fact of being shot at, of doing the things that men always do but doing them under fire. To use an image, when a group of seamen attempt to beach a boat in a raging surf, that is peace; but when they try it under enemy fire, that is war.

Motives for war, like the reasons for it, are also numerous; although they all fall under one or another of the headings of possession, power, principle, pleasure, prestige and human psychology. Thus, primitive men waged war for blood revenge, for possession of cattle (both as status symbols and as food), to capture women (for their labor as much as for the pleasure of their bodies), to acquire heads, to take slaves, to seize victims for human sacrifice, and, most common of all, to retaliate for some act of witchcraft by which an unfriendly tribe was believed to have caused death or disaster. The last motive is the immemorial drive for a scapegoat. All men— primitive and civilized—seek some "outsider" upon whom they can fasten the blame for all their sins, their failures and frustrations. In our own time, the most famous scapegoat was the Jews of Hitlerite Europe. Even today, we civilized people, just like the primitives beating "evil spirits" into the sea, require scapegoats. At the moment, our own "devil" seems to be the "Communists," while we "Capitalists" seem to supply the need in them.

The desire to dominate is another powerful stimulus for war, if it is not indeed the most potent of all. Nowadays we mercenary moderns are inclined to declare that all war is basically economic. This is not quite true. Rome, one of the most warlike societies of all time, seems to have been motivated chiefly by what the Roman historian Sallust and St. Augustine both described as *libido dominandi,* the lust for domination.

In addition to domination, modern governments declaring war are motivated by a desire for wealth, revenge, glory, prestige or adventure, or to unify the country and distract internal forces working for revolt, to stimulate revolt in the enemy country, to expand or to propagate a religion or a political ideal. Populations which willingly go to war, though not usually without being manipulated into a frenzy of hatred or fanaticism, do so because the individual men rushing to the colors are also inflamed with the hope of loot, land, higher wages, adventure, feminine approval or sexual satisfaction. On a nobler plane, they can be fired by loyalty to a religion, an ideal, a leader, a nation and even to their home and hearth. Men also join the colors to escape debt, marriage or boredom. *Esprit de corps,* pride in one's outfit or profession, is another motive; and finally, probably somewhere beneath all these drives, lies a man's nagging desire to test his own courage.

No one of these motives is ever solitary and unmixed. Most of the youths who joined the services on Pearl Harbor day had at least two: indignation at Japan's sneak attack that afternoon, and an unvoiced desire to prove their own manhood. Among the least warlike of the primitive tribes the sexual motive is uppermost. Wife-stealing or rape can cause a war, as can the elopement of a woman with a man from another group. In our war with Mexico, the governmental motive was expansionist, that of the Regular Army which won the war was professional pride, and among the volunteers who flocked to the various camps to riot, sicken and die, there was seldom anything nobler than the recruiters' promises of "roast beef, two dollars a day, plenty of whisky, golden Jesuses, and pretty Mexican girls."

The Crusades, those unique and fascinating expeditions to free the Holy Land, are generally thought to have been motivated by religious zeal. True, but there were other reasons, some unseen, but all equally powerful. Love of the Lord, for instance, shared precedence with hatred of the Saracen. Christendom was still reeling after its bloody clash at the hands of the Norse pirates, there had been plagues in 1094 and 1095, the feuding of the barons was threatening to rend the fabric of society, some princes were hopeful of carving out new kingdoms, the Eastern Empire was in danger of falling to Islam and the Italian city-states were eager to open profitable trade routes eastward. So many motives, and yet they were all fused into a single exalted purpose when Pope Urban II uttered his great rallying cry: "God wills it!"

It is an unpleasant but ineluctable fact of war that to be successful it must frequently be waged in an atmosphere of unreality and make-believe. On the surface, the Christians who took the Cross sought freedom for the Holy Land and absolution from their sins: actually, many of them were fired by lust or a spirit of adventure. Pope Urban truly did wish to do God's work on earth, but he also had the political motive of unifying Christendom. Yet, as long as the religious drive remained uppermost, and the Crusaders actually believed or thought that they believed in it, the Crusades were successful. But as the ordeal of the expeditions wore away zeal, as trial after trial exhausted exaltation (as it always and inevitably will do), then the baser, selfish motives became apparent and uppermost, cynicism set in, and glory gave way to disaster and disgrace.

When self-deception vanished, so also did success. In a word, there is simply no limit to self-delusion. Therefore, it would be well for governments and especially for men to ask themselves their true motives before taking the final drastic step of an appeal to arms. As a rule of thumb, it would probably be better to trust our own motives less and the other party's more; and so put a safety on our selfishness and suspicion, the twin triggers of aggression.

Once, however, the step has been taken, and the people are agreed that the cause is just, it must be understood that, as Clausewitz said: *"War is only a continuation of State policy by other means."*

For a modern state, then, there should be no other object of war but the fulfillment of some policy which diplomacy could not obtain. Once again, if diplomacy is the carrot of policy, then war is the stick. When a state cannot persuade, it will coerce. But always it should be for some reasonable object, some just goal. A war of extermination or annihilation, a life-or-death war in which the last American gunner perished destroying the last enemy pillbox, would be a senseless and immoral thing. Even the primitives understood this. Thus, when the warriors of some tribes returned triumphant from the battle, their women greeted them with the mournful chant: "Why have you killed our friends?" Even they were aware that war could never be its own object. This also was what Robert E. Lee meant when he said: "It is well that war is so terrible—or else we should grow too fond of it."

A war fought merely to kill or to annihilate our enemy would be no better than mass murder. War has to have a political object. Unfortunately, the very propaganda which modern nation-states employ to induce their people to hate the enemy has the effect of making them think in terms of annihilation. Americans are especially prone to conceive of war as a religious crusade, a kind of Armageddon in which the forces of good confront the minions of evil. We think always of "winning," but winning what? The political objective of World War II was certainly to free Europe, Germany as well as her conquered territories, from the Nazi yoke; and in the Pacific to do the same with Japan and her Fascist war lords. Instead, we proclaimed the misguided and vindictive policy of Unconditional Surrender, which, by discouraging opposition to the leadership in those countries, strengthened the Fascist hold on the people so that they fought on more desperately, thus prolonging the war at the cost of thousands of American lives.

Vindictiveness or blind vengeance can never be a political policy. It is insane to tell the enemy that he can hope for no terms, that he must throw himself upon the mercy of his conqueror. It is immoral to think of victory in terms of annihilation or obliteration, as though a grown man had the right to discipline a child by beating him to death. In World War II we won not a victory but an annihilation, one which left both Germany and Japan so utterly crushed and discredited that it was years before we could prop them up again as allies against Communism's aggressive moves to east and to west. We thought only in terms of military victory, ignoring the political truth that today's foe may be tomorrow's friend. The family of nations is much too interdependent ever to think of crushing or crippling one of them. The thrust of a war is against the enemy leadership, not the enemy people, not all of whom are ever responsible for or approve of enemy policy. But instead of waging war against the Fascist leadership, we waged it against the Fascist people. We did not seem to understand that if German and Japanese governments will come and go, Germany and Japan will remain. This, I think, was because of our crusading complex and our naive faith in "final solutions." Americans are forever saying, "Let's get this thing over with." But once you get "this thing" over with some new "thing" will inevitably arise to disturb you. This is because there are no "final solutions," no home run or long-bomb pass that ends the big game in victory, after which we can all go home and celebrate. Instead, there is always a new set of relationships just as tricky and frustrating as the old ones. As Edmund Burke said: "War never leaves where it found a nation."

Actually, this naive notion of "fighting to win" can be most harmful in its consequences. Certainly we do not fight to lose, but we also do not fight merely for "victory." Earlier in this study I compared war to sports, and they are similar in that they are both contests. Ultimately, however, they differ. The end of a sporting contest is victory or defeat, but the end of a war is to achieve some political object. Thus, in football, if Notre Dame defeats Michigan State she has achieved her object, and vice versa. But the true object of our war with the Axis was to liberate all the areas under the Axis yoke, to replace Fascist despotism with at least some form of free government. What happened? We did "win," we were "victorious" over the Axis powers; and to most Americans that "was it." Because we thought mere victory settled things, we were chagrined to see a new despotism—Communism—rush into the vacuum caused by the Axis collapse. Here was our old ally, Soviet Russia, becoming our new enemy. Here was Premier Stalin, a most astute if ruthless power-politician, taking the utmost political profit from military success. Eventually, of course, we did come to our senses, meeting Soviet Russia and then Communist China in the global confrontation called the Cold War. Our political and military leaders, if not our people, did finally learn that war is an instrument of state policy.

However, five years later in Korea, our people displayed the same foolish fascination for "victory." In Korea, the political objective was to prevent the conquest of non-Communist South Korea by Communist North Korea. In the end, this was what happened; but many Americans, disappointed because the North Koreans and their Chinese Communist allies did not lie crushed and prostrate at our feet, still think of Korea as a failure. They still do not understand that war is an instrument of state policy. A war is not fought to destroy an enemy but to deter him, to dissuade him from some course or policy which we consider inimical to our own. We did not need to crush King George III and all his subjects to gain our independence. All we needed to do was to demonstrate that it was more expensive for them to attempt to govern us than to allow us to govern ourselves.

Sometimes, of course, a purely political attitude toward war can seem cruel and inhuman. At Cold Harbor in June of 1864, Grant launched an assault on Lee's entrenched Confederates, and was repulsed with dreadful losses. Normally, Grant would have sent Lee a flag of truce, asking permission to rescue his wounded and bury his dead. However, 1864 was an election year, and Abraham Lincoln's dwindling political fortunes simply could not stand the admission of defeat which would be embodied in a flag of truce. So Grant made no such request, and Lee, equally alive to the political implications of the situation, forbade Federal rescue parties to bring in wounded. The result: four days and nights made hideous by the piteous crying of the stricken for help that never came. If, by this action, Grant seems to be a monster indifferent to the suffering of his men, how would history judge a general who caused the downfall of his commander-in-chief, thereby probably losing the war? If it is Lee who seems despicable, should he, by being more compassionate than his enemy, have thrown away the results of his victory? No, as William Tecumseh Sherman was soon to advise the citizens of Atlanta: "War is cruelty, and you cannot refine it." And it was General Sherman's very seizure of Atlanta the following September that gave Lincoln the electrifying victory required for his re-election.

War, then, to be sensible at all, has to be an instrument of policy, to be employed only when such other instruments as diplomacy, commercial pressure or the invocation of international procedures have failed.

It is the last argument, the last appeal of both men and nations. Once so useful, it is now, because of its great destructiveness, obviously less useful; perhaps, in the long run, even harmful. But war is so much the consequence of human attitudes and instincts that it does not seem likely to disappear until something wonderfully new happens to mankind. And that, I think, as Thomas More said of the advent of Utopia, will not be for some time.

INDEX

70 71 72 73 74 10 9 8 7 6 5 4 3 2 1

Please remember that this is a library book,
and that it belongs only temporarily to each
person who uses it. Be considerate. Do
not write in this, or any, library book.